Pretty Little DUMPSTER FIRES

FINDING WIT, WISDOM, AND LOVE IN AN IMPERFECT WORLD

M. J. Parisian

Published by Dream Life Publications

ISBN: 978-0-578-38208-1

Other books by M.J. Parisian

What We Know Now

This is How a Heart Breaks

To Live in this World

The Edge of Glory

For Linda,
From crying in the parking lot at STA,
to helping me find Frankfort,
Thank you.
Here is the book you always wanted...
xo, Pong

And for Jen,
Inspiration is all around us,
but this one was inspired by you.
Happy Birthday!

HOW IT STARTED

It all began with a small idea of starting a blog. I never liked that word—blog—but I knew in my heart it was what I was supposed to be doing at the time. Writing those posts was an outlet that filled something up in me. It allowed me to figure out life, motherhood, and my insatiable search for something more. And it allowed me to look at life through the lens of humor and see that we are all really going through the same things. My favorite thing in the world back then was to get a comment from one of those followers who could relate to what I was going through. I wrote about the struggles of motherhood, working, and losing a parent before I was ready. This book highlights my favorite posts from back then and reminds me of my "why" when I started.

One blog, two readers, and so many words to live by.

It gave me confidence in writing.

It gave me a voice.

It gave me an outlet that I so desperately wanted.

It gave me joy.

In the beginning, very few people even knew about my writing dreams. This quote from Brené Brown describes my early writing life so well:

"Our stories are not meant for everyone. Hearing them is a privilege, and we should always ask ourselves this before we share: "Who has earned the right to hear my story?"

That was then, this is now, and what remains are the words.

It wasn't until after my mom passed that I really started to look at my writing life as more than a secret for a select few. I began to want more than a three-hundred-word post and lit up at the idea of a full novel. I created characters that made me giggle and nod in agreement. Characters who were flawed the same way we all are, and in doing that, made us love them (and ourselves) more.

When I look back at some of the early posts, I cringe a little.

I complained... a lot.

But in the end, I would always dig out the change in perspective that we all need. Every time I hit "publish," my love for writing would grow.

Hearing that my words made a difference to someone is the fuel needed to keep the fire lit.

Some of you are wondering why I chose this title for a book that is ultimately about hope.

The idea for *Pretty Little Dumpster Fires* started with a texting conversation, and the cover is similar to a gif that is sent almost daily. The fact that I have a person I can reach out to when the world turns upside down and say WTF makes that problem infinitely smaller. The problem many of us have with our dumpster fires is we generally keep them to ourselves. Hush, hush. Keep it quiet. Don't let anyone in. But, when we keep all of that 'fire' inside, it tends to destroy the one thing you need most in this world: Yourself.

I like to think that my books are just long versions of these posts. With characters. And story lines.

The messages are the same now as they were back then:

We are all going through the same things.

You are not alone now, nor will you ever be.

Parenting is the hardest job on the planet. (Even for those with those picture-perfect Facebook profiles)

Facebook is fake news most of the time.

You are exactly where you need to be.

Going through the hard stuff is what makes you a better person.

You can get through anything with a few good friends. Even just one.

Love is love is love.

We all need to be kinder to ourselves.

Sometimes, all someone needs to hear is "I'm listening."

Dreaming is a privilege, and one most of us don't use enough.

I don't have all the answers, and my biggest flaw is to not take my own advice, ever. I'm making it up as I go along, but a few good readers happened to find me and made me believe I'm not alone in the world.

Neither are you.

The words that follow are truly words to live by, and I hope you find something that resonates with you. The posts make me smile and remind me of a time that was definitely busier, but also simpler. Every season is filled with growing pains, changes, transformations, and dumpster fires… and that's okay. It's how we know that we're moving forward. The second we are stagnant is when we should start worrying.

Be brave with your life… it really is the only one you have. If there was one recurring theme in 2021 for me, it is this: Life is short. Do not take one second for granted, and make sure the people you love know how you feel. Be kind to yourself, and wake up every day grateful for the next 86,400 seconds.

You got this.

xo, *mj*

COURAGE

For some reason, this word has been popping up in my life lately. It's not a word I take lightly, so when I see it or *feel* it... well, it sits with me for a while.

I started off my day at the rink, watching our adult skaters perform exhibitions in preparation for Adult Nationals. One woman, Francie, is over seventy, and out there skating to *Titanic* as if it were the Olympics. There were many others that, quite frankly, showed more courage in those twenty minutes than I have in the past two years. As I stood there, I realized that I just don't take chances anymore, and I wasn't really sure I ever had. There's something about putting yourself out there and taking a chance on something without one worry about what anyone else would say.

Three hours later I found myself at Sparrow Children's Hospital visiting Hannah, who is battling Hodgkin's Lymphoma, and I was faced with another form of courage. She slept most of the time so I was able to talk with her mom, who is the definition of courage. She is positive, full of faith and love, and confident that this is the way it's supposed to be. She knows that Hannah was chosen for this battle for whatever reason, and they have accepted this wholeheartedly. There were no complaints. There was no unhappiness. It was love and gratitude, and I am a better person having spent time with them today.

I would like to be a more courageous person. I would like to see how different life would be if I took more chances instead of playing it safe. I would be curious to see what would happen if I just once tried something new. In the past few weeks I have started doing a spin class that does give me butterflies before I get on the bike, so I keep going back.

It's not much, but it's a start. I would like to do more, but baby steps are about all I can do at this point. Who knows— maybe this class will get me on a roll and push me forward in other ways.

What can you do to add a little courage to your life?

I REALIZED
THAT I JUST
DON'T TAKE
CHANCES
ANYMORE, AND
I WASN'T
REALLY SURE I
EVER HAD.

HAPPY MOTHER'S DAY

I think by now we all know that I have this love/hate relationship with Mother's Day.

On the one hand...

Toby and the kids are extra nice that day.

Usually a meal is involved.

Everyone you see wishes you Happy Mother's Day.

My sister always gets me the best gifts. Spoils me rotten.

Spring is in the air.

But, on the other hand...

I still miss my mom.

I won't get bogged down on what I don't have without her, since I'm starting to learn that the best of her is still with me. I have her laugh. I have her smile. I have exceptional ~~parenting~~ mothering skills—just ask my kids or anyone at the rink. I take care of them all.

My office is a lot like her office was: Always filled with someone wanting to hang out or needing advice. Sometimes they just want to vent. On the really bad days, they'll shut the door and cry.

So I sit and listen, giving them what they need, whether it's a hug, simple advice, or a kick in the pants. I witnessed this gift in my mother when I was in high school, and now I see it in myself. It's as if she is really still here.

But she's not.

The one way I know my mom is still watching over me is the mere fact that I am surrounded by some of the best moms I know.

My friends.

As I was walking tonight, I had this overwhelming feeling of being blessed with friendship. These moms are the ones who have held me up over the years.

Laughed with me.

Cried with me.

Give me hope and support when I need it, and of course a kick in the pants too.

We've swapped recipes and cookbooks.

We check up on each other's kids.

We always trade books.

We do breakfast, lunch, dinner, and movies.

Drinks are a given, and 'wine-ing' is allowed.

In a nutshell, I am blessed.

So to all you moms (and some of you aren't even moms yet): Thank you. Thank you for making this thing we call life worth living. Thank you for getting me through the hard days and making the easy days more fun.

We are all blessed to have each other, for certain.

Thanks, Mom...

THE ONE WAY I KNOW
MY MOM IS STILL
WATCHING OVER ME
IS THE MERE FACT
THAT I AM
SURROUNDED BY
SOME OF THE BEST
MOMS I KNOW.

My friends.

POPSIE

As I'm sitting here today, I realize how little I talk about my dad. It's almost as if he doesn't exist, at least in my little online world. That is so sad, because we all know what my mom meant to me... and yet we know very little about my dad.

So, on this Father's Day Weekend, we celebrate Popsie...

POPSIE'S TOP TEN

1. Even though we don't always see it, Popsie is one of the most religious men on the planet. He gets to the shop every morning around five thirty a.m. so he can say a rosary before the boys get in. He has never not done this.

2. He had one true love in his life—my mom—and it has never entered his mind that he should remarry. They celebrated their 46th anniversary the year she died.

3. He is a staunch Republican and will dislike someone simply for being a Democrat (hence my first line in #1). And I am not kidding. If you want to get him riled up, ask him about Democrats, but be prepared to hear some cursing. It's not for the weak... Or children.

4. He is an avid watcher of all things horse racing. Don't call him if a horse race is on—or even *about* to come on. He just wants to focus.

5. Popsie LOVES sports—especially his grandkids—but HATES refs. There isn't a ref in Lansing that hasn't been yelled at by my dad. It embarrasses the hell out of me, but most people seem to think it's funny. It's a little cringy.

6. Music is one of the things he and I have in common. Ever

since I was little, we have shared this love of the same kind of music. It always made me happy when I found the perfect music for a skater and thought, *ohhh, Dad would love this.*

7. My dad is unable to pass up a sale. A four-dollar shirt at Kohls (schmedium, no less)? Sure! Ten-pound can of coffee? You betcha. It doesn't matter what the sale is, really, he just wants to cash it in.

8. My dad loves, loves, LOVES going to the movies. He even rates them like Gene Siskel, himself. It was very rare for a movie to get a ten, but on those rare occasions, we made sure we saw it.

9. Up until they closed, Old Country Buffet was his favorite place to eat. This was THE place to go for birthdays or any celebration. It's the only place where you can get all-you-can-eat bacon *and* make your own sundae. My kids share this love with him.

10. He is one of the most generous people I know and would give you the shirt off your back if you needed it.

I really could go on and on with small tidbits about him that would make you smile or even giggle. The truth is, he is an amazing man who has worked hard his whole life. His business started out at Vic Garmyn and Son—and he was the son. I've always said I got my work ethic from my dad and my spending habits from my mom.

If I didn't have one, I couldn't have the other.

So, that's my Pops in a nutshell. I hope you're lucky enough to have met him at some point, but if not just know he's a generous and lovable old man who loves his family more than anything, who has taught me a great deal about life.

HE IS AN

amazing

MAN WHO
HAS WORKED
HARD HIS
WHOLE LIFE.

BLESSED

Well this is new… writing in the hospital. But all is quiet—at least, Blake is quiet—so I had some time to think, because I'm pretty sure that sleep will elude me here.

I was telling someone today that this has to be, hands down, the absolute worst week of Blake's life. That's not an exaggeration, just a fact. He has been poked and prodded, ultrasounded and cat-scanned. He hasn't eaten since Wednesday morning, and it's Friday night as I write this. Contestants on *Survivor* eat more than he has.

But for some reason, I am so at peace right now. Probably because he is, but also because Toby and I have literally been text bombed all week. Family and friends wondering how he is… wondering how we are… and what they can do to help.

It's overwhelming to think about the circle of people around us, and it reminds me of how lucky and blessed we really are—even as I write this in the hospital.

I know this too shall pass, because my mom always said it would. But also because it's true.

The bad times always pass.

The good ones do too.

That is the one thing we can always count on in this crazy world.

That, and the fact that Blake will never do anything half-way. Like… *ever*.

Have a fabulous weekend, my friends.

P.S. If you're reading this and didn't have a clue, Blake is going to be just fine.

THE BAD TIMES
ALWAYS PASS.
THE GOOD ONES
DO TOO.

THAT IS THE ONE
THING WE CAN
ALWAYS COUNT ON
IN THIS CRAZY
WORLD.

STRUGGLES

Schedules are hectic lately and only getting worse for the next few weeks.

Homework and events are increasing.

Lacrosse schedules change by the hour, somedays.

Work is in that difficult spot of being unsatisfying and annoying at the same time. Which is fun.

So, I took another personal day today, and while I still have to go in tonight, I have the "school day" to myself. And it just so happens to be sunny and 70 degrees. Quite literally.

I've had an issue lately of squandering away any free time I have, since it's so scarce. I'll find myself watching an hour of TV and not having a clue as to what was even on. I'll sit with a cup of coffee in the morning and just let my mind run through the usual loop of negative thinking. Or my personal favorite: I'll get to school thirty minutes early so I can play Candy Crush till I'm out of lives.

You know... super useful things.

When I woke up today, I knew work was not going to be on the agenda, unless you count writing on my deck. In shorts, T-shirt, and sunglasses.

Once I decided I would be home today, I did something that I usually don't do: I sat down and tried to figure out what would really make me happy. At the same time I read an email I got from *Notes from the Universe* explaining the ten things people take for granted.

#9: How easy life is when they stop struggling.

And it hit me instantly—I've been resisting everything from schedules to work, and even sleep. Poor me... life is busy and hectic and messy. Oh sure, I have the same thoughts as those negative people on Facebook we make fun of, but I just keep them hidden. They're in my closet of bad thoughts.

Poor, poor me.

All I have wanted lately—craved really—is someone to take care of me. Take care of my messy, complicated, amazing life. In short, I miss my mom. I miss the feeling of comfort I had knowing she could take care of anything and always make my life easy. Mother's Day is always a double-edged sword.

So in looking back to #9, I didn't struggle when she was around. Life was just easier.

In that moment, I knew that life wasn't about being *without* struggle, and resisting all of it is where the problem lies.

"Bravery can only come from having something to be brave about.... We are only as great as our struggles."
— Katherine Center

Looking at your life—the good, the bad, and the ugly—and not only accepting it, but being grateful is where happiness resides.

Now, I'm not saying that it's easy, but at least you know that you're not alone.

Everyone has struggles.

Everyone has pain.

Everyone has something in their life they want to change.

And everyone can be brave.

I hope you have a wonderful and messy and chaotic day. It means you're still living.

Be grateful.

I KNEW THAT LIFE
WASN'T ABOUT BEING
WITHOUT STRUGGLE,
AND RESISTING ALL
OF IT IS WHERE THE
PROBLEM LIES.

BESTEST

True, you won't find this word in Webster's, but it doesn't stop me from using it all the time. Probably not as much as I should lately, but I'm working on that starting here. Trying to see the best in any situation is a tough skill to learn, and once you do, it's even tougher to maintain.

Sadly, I can only relate it to a diet.

When I look back, I can clearly see that my moods—like my diet—are on some sort of crazy mood pendulum, swinging from really happy to my-life-has-no-purpose. Am I bipolar? Probably not, but I just lose focus of the big picture from time to time and slip into seeing only the bad around me.

When you take the time to just count your blessings, no matter how small, life really isn't so bad. I know, I know, easier said than done.

So taking a cue from my favorite website, I'm going to copy one of their ideas and make a list of Best Evers.

- **Best Song**: "What a Wonderful World" by Louis Armstrong. Yes, it's corny, but it's true. This was our wedding song, and to this day it will bring a smile to my face. I will have to say that "At Last" by Etta James is a very close second.

- **Best Book**: Really? I have to pick just one? Well most of you could probably guess that it would be the last Harry Potter, *The Deathly Hallows*. I have had an obsession with Harry since I started reading them so many years ago. Close second will have to be *Charlotte's Web*. There is still something about that story that literally made me want to live on a farm when I was little. Love.

- **Best Movie**: *You've Got Mail.* If I ever win the lottery, I will reopen The Shop Around the Corner... and add a coffee shop with it. Love, love, love.

- **Best Life Moment**: This is the hardest one because there are so many!

  o I would have to say that the first time you hold your child is one of the most amazing moments God could ever give you.

  o Walking down the aisle towards Toby who couldn't stand still because he was so nervous.

  o Writing the last paragraph in my first book. It was a moment when I realized how important it is not to give up on something you want to do.

  o Being surrounded by friends, love, tears, and laughter on the night of my mom's funeral. It was sad and beautiful at the same time.

- **Best Advice**: Make all of your choices out of love, not fear. Don't do anything because you're afraid of what will happen if you don't. Yes, you need to be wise, but when you start living in fear, you really just stop living.

So that's it. Start today to see the best in your life.... even if it's just the best cup of coffee you've ever had. Starting small—baby steps—is sometimes the best way.

IT WAS A
MOMENT WHEN I
REALIZED HOW
IMPORTANT IT IS
NOT TO GIVE UP
ON SOMETHING
YOU WANT TO DO.

INSPIRED

Inspired... that's my word of the day.

I'm hoping it lasts for more than just a day though.

I've been looking everywhere for it. High and low. In desk drawers. In file folders. Even in the cookie jar.

It couldn't be found anywhere. At least not where I was looking.

Then a friend of mine said she was doing a speaking engagement today for a teacher's conference, so I decided to leave work early and go see her.

Truth be told, I would pretty much cross state lines to watch her read the phone book. She's *that* good.

And it's not so much what she's saying all the time... it's how she says it and the meaning behind the words. She is a children's book author, a teacher, wife and mother, daughter, and friend. So many things to so many people. In fact, she has inspired me to write another top ten list.

TOP TEN THINGS ALLISON HAS TAUGHT ME:

1. Being real and honest about who you truly are is a beautiful thing. So many people out there are trying to fit into a mold of who they think they should be (myself included), so it's amazing to be around someone who is 100% completely owning who they are.

2. Beauty can be found everywhere.

3. Public speaking doesn't have to be scary or boring. She is brilliant.

4. Real people attract real friends who are really nice.

5. It's okay to have issues, and if you can share them in a way to make someone else feel like they're not alone... well, that's just perfect.

6. She is funny, wise, and likes to curse as much as I do.

7. Be nice to everyone (even the people you might not like).

8. Home is where your heart is.

9. Taking chances is necessary for growth.

10. It's the little things in life that truly make a difference. How you treat people and live your life will come back to you every time. Be kind.

So you can see why my inspiration is jumping off the page now? I hope you can all find something to be inspired about this weekend.

IT'S THE LITTLE
THINGS IN LIFE
THAT TRULY MAKE A
DIFFERENCE. HOW
YOU TREAT PEOPLE
AND LIVE YOUR LIFE
WILL COME BACK
TO YOU EVERY TIME.

Be kind.

INSPIRATION

This might be my favorite subject of all time.

One never knows when they are going to be inspired and determined to rid themselves of the nasty feelings inside for lighter and brighter ones. It literally can happen at any given moment. Usually, there is a reason—a person, place, or thing—for the feeling of *okay, I can do this* to capture your heart. And sometimes, it's just that feeling of being sick of the stupid voices in your head that will push you into a positive momentum.

This is a combination of both.

Plus, Evan goes back to school tomorrow, which means that Blake goes back the following week, and everyone knows that structure and I go waaaay back. Structure is my BFF. I don't think I'm alone in this, although everyone I talk to says "it's too soon to go back to school" or "I'm not ready for summer to be over."

These are not my people.

Am I ready to start fighting with Evan over grades? No, but at least it's not about who gets the xBox next, and for how long. I know that fall isn't going to bring that world peace feeling I'm longing for, but at least I won't be battling the guilt of leaving my kids at home while I work all summer. So at least I have that going for me.

Tonight, I finally picked up Anna Quindlen's *Lots of Candles, Plenty of Cake* probably because I was internally seeking some inspiration. And she never disappoints. After the first two pages, I literally thought to myself, "Why am I not writing about all this crazy stuff in my head? Surely there is someone who can relate to me?"

Anyone?

But it really doesn't matter if no one replies, because I know you're out there. And even if it's not about summer ending, there's something else going on in your life, and it's just nice to know that we're all going through some sort of challenge.

We need to stick together at times like this.

And we definitely need our inspiration.

"WHY AM I NOT WRITING ABOUT ALL THIS CRAZY STUFF IN MY HEAD?

SURELY THERE IS SOMEONE WHO CAN RELATE TO ME?"

MORTIFIED

A friend of mine has been listening to my parenting horror stories for a while, saying they're the best birth control ever. So jokingly I told her last week that she doesn't know mortified until she has kids.

She promises that it'll be the title of her book someday.

It's become my mission to give her the dirt so she will know exactly what she's getting into when they make that decision. You literally have to be crazy to have kids. Yes, they bring a lot of joy to our lives, and quite frankly, life might be a little b-o-r-i-n-g without them, but good Lord, do they have to teach us such humility? There isn't a day that goes by that I don't sprout at least one new gray hair because of them.

Here is today's email to my childless friend...

We are running late as usual this morning, and Evan decides he wants to drive to school.

Great!

He finds his favorite Mac Miller song, so I can listen to rap on the way.

Super!

He goes to back out of the garage and bumps into the shelves in front of us. He's in DRIVE... in our garage.

Excellent!

Screaming, "GODDAMMIT, GO BACKWARDS," is probably not my shining moment in parental advice. Not to mention I threaten Blake that if he tells Dad I'll take his iPod away.

You can stop laughing now, because it will happen to you someday.

You don't know mortified till you're a parent.
#mortified.

... I thought it might just make some of you others giggle too. And for the record, if any of you tell Toby, I'll take your iPod away as well.

Sidenote: This childless friend from long ago ended up having triplets. Then I was her nanny. Pretty sure that's the definition of irony.

LIFE MIGHT BE A
B-O-R-I-N-G
WITHOUT THEM,
BUT GOOD LORD,
DO THEY HAVE TO
TEACH US SUCH
HUMILITY?

MISS LIST

*[On June 26, 2012, Nora Ephron passed away after a battle
with leukemia that she kept mostly hidden. As you will read, I
adored her...]*

In my opinion, Nora Ephron was a genius. Not only were her
books funny, honest, and witty, she also wrote two of my
Top Ten favorite movies: *Sleepless in Seattle* and *You've Got
Mail*.

Her writing was real and honest, with an Erma Bombeck
flavor to her stories. As a reader, writer, and woman, I felt
seen and understood after reading one of her books. Her
movies? Well, they just captured my heart.

Near the end of her last book, *I Remember Nothing, and
Other Reflections,* she included two lists: What I Won't Miss
was one, and What I Will Miss was the other. Because of
copyright laws I'm not going to print them here, but if you
get a chance, google them and enjoy. In the meantime
though, I challenge you to make your own lists of what you'd
miss and what you wouldn't should you have a week to live.
I believe when we look at time in such a limited capacity, our
true love for things in life is instantly clear.

Here are mine...

WHAT I WON'T MISS
- working
- drying my hair
- emptying the dishwasher
- 90 degrees and humid

- nasty customers
- back pain and headaches
- root canals, or any dental work for that matter
- counting calories, or any diet-related chore
- insomnia
- voicemail
- traffic
- grocery shopping

WHAT I WILL MISS

- Toby, Evan, and Blake (Goldie too, if I'm being honest)
- my family (every crazy last one of them)
- music
- baking cookies
- reading
- writing
- hot showers in the winter
- down blankets
- cool summer evenings on the deck
- crisp fall days
- laughing with friends
- movies
- teaching someone how to skate
- giving advice
- buttered popcorn
- ice. cold. beer.
- the perfect spring day
- the text that will make you giggle when you're having a horrible day
- inappropriate Thursdays

- my work family
- the friends who have never left my side (you know who you are)
- laughter through tears
- Siesta Key
- Seeing happiness on my kids' faces

I know there are many more I'll think of later for each list, but it's a good place to start. I like that my Miss List is longer than my Won't Miss list.

I think that says I'm on the right track.

WHEN WE LOOK AT
TIME IN SUCH A
LIMITED CAPACITY,

OUR TRUE LOVE FOR
THINGS IN LIFE IS
INSTANTLY CLEAR.

GRATITUDE

I'm feeling like I'm in the movie *Finding Nemo*, and I'm the dad. And instead of looking for Nemo, though, I'm searching for gratitude. I know, I know, this is what I preach, the base of what I know to be true and real, for the past few years.

And yet I'm searching.

It seems this year has been about growth for me, and growing pains are hell.

With a broken-family Thanksgiving and a hockey tournament on Friday, life seems to be throwing me a curveball. God is saying "find your gratitude in this mess," and I can finally see that. I have never been so anxious to get a few days over with, and yet I really don't want to be that person anymore who wishes the days away. I want to try and enjoy the process of cooking for my family and spending time with them. I want them to say it was an awesome Thanksgiving, filled with good food and new traditions.

I don't want them to say 'that's the turkey from *Christmas Vacation*.'

Life is messy and rarely goes how we planned it. If we can get through the tough times with gratitude in our hearts, then we can expect to be happier more often. And if we can remember to stay in the moment instead of stressing about the future, we will also be happier all the time.

Isn't that really what it's all about... being happier?

My wish for you is to have a wonderful Thanksgiving, spent with those you love, wrapped in the warm blanket of gratitude.

"In the end, though, maybe we must all give up trying to pay back the people in this world who sustain our lives. In the end, maybe it's wiser to surrender before the miraculous scope of human generosity and to just keep saying thank you, forever and sincerely, for as long as we have voices."

— Elizabeth Gilbert

And just like that, I can see gratitude.

IF WE CAN GET
THROUGH THE
TOUGH TIMES WITH
GRATITUDE IN OUR
HEARTS, THEN WE
CAN EXPECT TO BE
HAPPIER MORE
OFTEN.

TEAMWORK

Well, in 2013 fashion, we have had another one of those weeks.

There are so many different things going on right now, and it reminds me of my statement back in December: Crazy is the new normal.

This weekend's events with hockey seem to be sitting with me and bringing up a very important message that I think we all need to be reminded of from time to time.

TEAMWORK.

I often think of the scene from *Miracle* where the players are asked who they play for, and after countless ladder drills, it's Mike Eruzione who announces, "United States of America." It's one of those perfect moments in movies that can inspire because we know instantly that was what he was looking for the whole time.

Blake's team has been struggling for the past couple weeks, mostly because they had forgotten they are a group of boys playing for one goal. Not individual players who think they can do it on their own. I'm pretty sure the lesson was learned last night as we watched them warm up by themselves, and heard about a pre-game locker room pep talk from each player... no coach involved. Listening to Blake—who was clearly moved—talk about it made my eyes water with pride.

And an 11-1 win is a pretty strong statement from a team.

"I love my team," he said, wrapping it up.

Me too, Blaker, me too.

But of course, this lesson isn't just for the team. Our lives—our *goal*—seem to be about handling one thing after another, preventing the almighty stay-in-the-moment feeling we're I'm seeking. Some of us are handling BIG things and some of us are handling smaller things, and I always pretend I can handle problems on my own much better than sharing with a friend. I am the classic loner when life is in chaos. I stop answering the phone, make many excuses to get out of social events, and hide behind work. I try to avoid people at all costs so I don't have to pretend to be happy. In this world when everyone is trying to be perfect and appearances mean everything, I know I hate to be the Eyore in the group. It's such an ungrateful feeling, and beating it alone is just what I've always done.

When I look back on my life, I can only wonder why I do this to myself. Teamwork can apply to life, too, and our friends and family are the teammates who can carry the load and support us when we fall. We don't have to be alone when we're "losing" and instead, we should be rallying with people who are on our team... allowing them to help us through the game of life.

"Alone we can do so little; together we can do so much."
— Helen Keller

I am glad I have you all on my team.

TEAMWORK CAN
APPLY TO LIFE,
TOO, AND OUR
FRIENDS AND
FAMILY ARE THE
TEAMMATES WHO
CAN CARRY THE
LOAD AND SUPPORT
US WHEN WE FALL.

LOVE AND MARRIAGE

Usually, these two words go together like a couple, hand in hand, but I have actually come to realize they mean two different things. I believe that love is the heart-thumping, giddy, romantic feeling we have when we meet *the one*. Love is that feeling we're reminded of when seeing two people meet at the end of the aisle. Love is in the moments of vows, kisses, and beautiful dresses.

Marriage, on the other hand, is something completely different. It is the day-to-day life you will build together, knowing that at the end of each day, no matter what happens, someone's got your back.

And every wedding I attend, I find they make me reevaluate and analyze my own life and marriage. Here is what I have come up with:

When they say '*Do you take this person for better or for worse, in good times and in bad...*' they mean it. On any wedding day, it's impossible to foresee life unfolding with its ups and downs, and know how much those two words will challenge you: I do.

Wedding days are very similar to a baby being born. The moment is magical perfection, full of hope, promise, and of course, love. The amount of hard work, dedication, and commitment is not brought up. A marriage cannot survive if you can't take that person and still love them on their "for worse" days. I used to have a saying when I coached: When you are taking a test, you should be able to pass that test, even on your worst day.

The same rule applies with a marriage. You may not like them even on their worst days, but you do still love them.

You must take the good *with* the bad and accept them, flaws and all.

And then you drop to your knees and pray they do the same for you.

So it comes down to this... these words DO belong together. One cannot exist without the other. Without love, there would be no marriage. Some marriages never make it out of the gate because as soon as that giddy feeling is worn off, there is a whole lotta work. Too much of the focus has been put on the picture-perfect wedding and not the marriage.

Some days are good ones. Some need a little attention. And some are filled with the content, warm, fuzzy moments, and you think: I chose wisely.

It's called life.

And this is dedicated to the one who agreed to a lifetime with me.

And this is dedicated to the one who agreed to a lifetime with me.

LIGHTS

During the Christmas season, my mom used to go a little crazy.

You may think I'm kidding, but if you knew her, you know exactly what I mean. Christmas was, hands-down, her favorite time of year when she could shop and decorate to her little heart's desire.

And by decorate, I mean Snow Village.

For those of you who have no idea what Snow Village is, let me explain: It is another level of collecting. I'm not sure if it's still popular, but I am sure there's someone who still collects the houses and stores, trees, cars, people, animals, fake snow, and don't forget those little light fixtures that go inside each home.

My mom built a village every. freaking. year. She always joked that I would get the Snow Village after she was gone, because she knew I wouldn't take the time to put it up. The mere idea of setting up the village gave me hives.

However, I have to say... after all these years, I kinda miss it.

Going over there in the evening and viewing it all lit up was almost magical. The houses looked so cozy with the soft glow of lighting, and it always reminded me of hot chocolate and warm cookies. It's the same feeling you get watching Hallmark movies.

My mom had that light inside and out. It's the magic dust that is sprinkled on some people during this time of year.

Today—because of the Michigan drearies—I am reminded of that soft glow of lighting, and it got me thinking.... can we cast a light within ourselves for the people around us or even

43

ourselves? Can we light up our day just by being "lighter" to the people around us? Lighter in our thoughts? Lighter in our presence?

I am going to try since today is Monday, and dreary, and simply because I know it will make a difference.

Is your light on?

CAN WE
LIGHT UP
OUR DAY
JUST BY
BEING
"LIGHTER"
TO THE
PEOPLE
AROUND US?

OLD AND RESTLESS

There are so many things going on in life right now, and I am constantly feeling the need to hit the Do-Over button. If only there was a magic lever in life that would either take us back to the beginning or propel us to a future date when life wasn't so complicated.

As if a future time like that even existed.

I find myself lately wondering where the time has even gone. Forget about the future... What happened to the past? Was I so busy with kids and daily life that I didn't notice that time was flying by? I have pictures—so many pictures—that document our kids' happy childhood, but somehow, that part of our life is gone.

Everything feels different now.

The life I'm in right now seems to be one that is by default. One that wasn't necessarily a vision of mine, but rather, one that I have settled for. When you're in the hustle and bustle of "busy life" you merely get through the days, exhausted, drained, and grateful for the bed at night. You don't dream of something different, because that would seem ungrateful, and no one ever wants to be ungrateful when it comes to family life.

Being a mom requires you to put everyone else first, and we do that with pride. It's a badge of honor to be baking at midnight because someone forgot to tell you about the class party.

Or waiting in line to buy an entire homeroom breakfast burritos at Mickey D's.

Or sewing together the shoulder pads five times in a month.

Or the countless trips to school and back, every day for 12+ years.

Or sitting in doctor's offices, hospitals, and in rocking chairs in the middle of the night.

We've all done it and should be proud.

However, it's all changing now, and we have to find ourselves again. The one who used to dream about life and the pursuit of goals. The one who wants more than just a job to pay the bills, but something that feels like a calling.

And maybe it's just me feeling this way, but I don't think so.

This restlessness feels like this season of my life is nearing the end, and something bigger (and hopefully better) is on the horizon. Now is the time to maybe dust off the journal and start writing about what we really want our lives to look like. What does the perfect day look like on paper?

Write it down.

And no, it shouldn't be drinking and baking all day. I may or may not have had to cross that one out.

The main fact is some of us are hiding behind our daily life because we forgot how to dream. I know I did. But that has changed, and I'm in full-on reinvention mode. I am trying new things. Trying, for the first time in my life, to ignore what I perceive others are thinking about me, and just doing things that belong on a grateful list.

Which I write every day.

I know this isn't for everyone, and we all have a pace we're comfortable with, but if you're the tiniest bit restless like I am, then follow along. I haven't been ignoring this blog, but rather, a bit uninspired to write the same stuff over and over again.

I finally feel like I have something different to say to you, and I hope you'll be listening.

Word.

WHAT DOES THE PERFECT DAY LOOK LIKE ON PAPER?

ROLES

What role are you playing in life? If your life were a sitcom or—heaven forbid—a drama, what would your part be?

Are you the dutiful but wisecracking wife?

Are you the struggling parent trying to keep it all together?

Or are you the one who has the perfect life with a daily dose of humor?

The biggest problem with the roles we play is sometimes it's just that: We're *playing* them. Acting the part, instead of feeling whatever it is we're supposed to be feeling. Our identity becomes so wrapped up in the role that you lose the part of you that is real.

You following me?

Sometimes, we get so stuck in the role we're playing, constantly in character, and we forget the world is going to change, grow, and move on without us.

Motherhood (or parenthood) is the biggest role in many of our lives. And please don't misunderstand me... that role *is* the most important role you will ever have. However, it is all-consuming, and as the kids get older, the role changes drastically. That is the space I'm in right now. I'm still a mom, and will ALWAYS love being a mom, but the role isn't 24/7 like it used to be. Ten years ago was a lot different than it is now, and I'll admit I was a little unprepared for how quickly it all changed. I think I loved the role ten years ago because I didn't have to think too much about the rest of life. It was just all about the kids and what they needed.

Sure, I found myself resentful sometimes... okay *a lot of the time*, but I also took a lot of pride in motherhood.

So I come back to this: We are not the roles we are playing. Those roles are a part of us, but they shouldn't define us. The things that define us are the things that will always be a part of our lives no matter what else changes.

The hobbies.

The likes and dislikes.

The things we do when no one is around.

If you're wandering around, wondering what to do, start digging in to see what interests you. Check out the people in your life who inspire you and find out what they are doing. Take a class. Join a club. Become involved in a cause you believe in. Volunteer.

You never know what new role will fit till you try it out. Will it be easy? Absolutely not. It will be hard and challenge you, but that is when you figure out who you really are. The best of you is found on the other side of your comfort zone.

Life is good.

And you are worth the effort.

THE BEST OF YOU
IS FOUND ON THE
OTHER SIDE OF
YOUR COMFORT
ZONE.

WHAT I KNOW FOR SURE

I was given Oprah's book at Christmas, *What I Know For Sure*, and loved every word of it. My favorite part of her magazine was found on the last page—her wisdom at the end—and I would always feel like I had learned something from reading them. Many times it felt like she was reading my mind.

And today I got the nudge to write again, and while it's been a lot of time away, I feel like it was a necessary break. Sometimes we have to find new things to talk about or we run the risk of falling into the endless black hole of redundancy.

I know I'm getting older, but repeating myself isn't a road I want to go down anytime soon.

So I thought I'd start off this year with my own list of things I know for sure. It's a work in progress, and I know it might be different next year, but that is how life works... which leads me to my first thing.

- The only thing we can count on is nothing stays the same. Nothing. If there is anything I've learned lately is that what we have right here—right now—could all be different tomorrow. Sometimes they're good changes, and sometimes they're bad. Rarely is it in our control. Best to learn to go with the flow.

- Friends make the world go around. I think my friends are the reason I can stay sane in a crazy world. We joke. We cry. We bitch. We protect. We love. We listen. We advise. It doesn't matter what it is, my friends are there for me. I am beyond blessed to have the best of them too. Friends that would bail me out of jail. Friends sitting beside me in said jail. Friends that understand I'm not perfect. Friends that laugh ~~at~~ with me. Friends that read my blog and ask for more.

- Creativity > Laziness. Even the greatest day-long-*Scandal*-binge-watching-marathon isn't as good as writing one really good paragraph/scene/chapter. It just isn't. Doing something productive always wins. But if you can learn to be productive/creative while watching *Scandal*... Well, shut the front door. You got yourself perfection.

- You will never be prepared for bad news. How could you? We can't be those kinds of people who walk around expecting the worst all the time. We believe, we hope, we dream. So when the bad news comes, it usually sneaks up on you and flips your world upside down. It changes us and our reality, giving us a different perspective than we had before. We will learn to believe, hope, and dream again, but it will always be different than before. It just takes time.

- Resentment will eat you alive. Raise your hand if you cling to resentment like a fuzzy warm blanket. Yeah, me too. I'm learning, though, that life is too short, and eventually all that resentment is just hurting yourself. Like drinking poison and expecting the other person to get sick. Let it go...

- What someone thinks of you is only their business. This one is a work in progress for me, for sure. I am the ultimate people pleaser. If it were an Olympic sport, I'd be a multiple gold medalist. Constant worrying about what others think is the quickest way to resentment. See what I just did there? Anyways, start listening to yourself about what you want... or who to be with... or what to write about. At the end of the day, you are the only one you have to please. People will naturally come and go in your life... Pretending to be something or someone else is just making you miserable. Miserable = resentment.

- Giving is better than receiving. Once a month I pay for the person behind me at Starbucks. It's never a big amount, but the joy I get from doing that one thing lasts me the whole day. I have never regretted doing or giving something to someone, and I truly believe your heart grows when you do.

- There really are some words to live by. Here are just a few: Joy. Calm Strength. Peace. Courage. Love. Laughter. Grat-itude. Find one word to guide you each day. It will change the way you think and live.

- Being kind is better than being right. Anyone who's been married longer than a year knows this. #word

- No matter how old you get, you will always need your mom. It's been 11 1/2 years since I've seen my mom. I know she's there, watching over me, but sometimes that's not good enough. I need parenting advice in the worst way right now, and relying on myself isn't cutting it. I know I don't have a choice, and muddling through it is all I've got, but a sign would be really good, Mom. Just a little sign.

Well that's it. What I know for sure. Is it the same as what you know? Probably not. But I hope you will take the time to at least think about what your list would be.

THERE REALLY ARE SOME WORDS TO LIVE BY. HERE ARE JUST A FEW:

Joy.

Calm.

Strength.

Peace.

Courage.

Love.

Laughter.

MY PEOPLE

Taylor Swift has her squad.

Oprah has Gayle.

Mark Wahlberg has his entourage.

And I have my people.

In this day and age, when life is moving quickly, and you don't know what day it is half the time, it's nice to know that a girlfriend is just a text away. I know, I know, we're all obsessed with our phones, and everyone just wants to unplug!

But not me. No way. I get nervous when my phone battery gets down to twenty percent.

If it weren't for my phone, I wouldn't have been able to get through this week.

Like, for real.

A simple text message, or a year-long group text, can literally change the course of my day. You see, on the other end of that text is someone I treasure. Someone I can bond with over Whole30 Hell. Someone who gets my writing struggles. Someone who is also waiting for the end of a championship game that has gone into overtime and a shoot-out. Someone who makes me giggle, and someone who knows when I'm crying.

I don't think it's antisocial—unless you're at a restaurant with a friend across from you—because you're communicating and sharing your life with your people.

And everyone needs a tribe. I love my husband just as much as the next person, but it's my girlfriends who have gotten me through life.

The nitty-gritty stuff.

The stuff that men just wouldn't understand.

The ~~diets~~ nutrition resets.

Stuff like waxing, mothering, and *Criminal Minds*.

Scandal textathons.

Books! Men just don't get books.

Fear of failing at motherhood.

Fear of failing at writing.

Fear of just failing.

I don't know any woman who is able to handle motherhood, work (or not), schedules, meals, family, games, and travel without her friends around her. If you see your friends every day, then you're one of the lucky ones. I am not that fortunate. But I am blessed to have a list of friends I can text at any moment to share my life with.

So be thankful today. Thankful for the women who just get who you are and still like you. Life goes fast, and I know we are only here for a short time. Don't hold grudges or pass judgements... you sometimes don't know what someone else is going through. Instead, take the high road and be kind to everyone. Not everyone will be a part of your tribe and that's okay. Haters are going to hate, and you'll always be able to find someone who can criticize everything you do. It's okay. You don't need their opinion, but you can still be nice.

It's taken me a while to get to this point. Like I said earlier, I wouldn't have gotten through the week without my peeps, so perhaps I'm feeling a bit mushy right now.

Take a moment and text a friend. Make them giggle... tomorrow is another day, and they need it.

I LOVE MY
HUSBAND JUST
AS MUCH AS THE
NEXT PERSON,
BUT IT'S MY
GIRLFRIENDS
WHO HAVE
GOTTEN ME
THROUGH LIFE.

COMMAS

Comma — n 1. *the punctuation mark(,) indicating a slight pause in the spoken sentence and used where there is a listing of items or to separate a nonrestrictive clause or phrase from a main clause.*

After I spent way too many hours on a middle school play program, someone proofing it for me became the comma police, to the point where I felt like she wanted a comma after every word.

I, felt, defeated, by, a, simple, punctuation, mark.

Thankfully, I have a group of fabulous women surrounding me who know the difference between logic and a case of extreme punctuationitis.

Not that there's anything wrong if you have it.

However, when I get a long list the night before it goes to press, I tend to get a little cranky. And of course I have to ask myself, 'What is this comma trying to teach me?' I'm old enough to know that when something presents itself to me with such a force, an area in my life needs attention.

God knocks in funny ways.

All day yesterday I kept asking myself, where do I need to pause? Where do I need to make some separations in my life? And of course, this comes to me in a week where there are no breaks, and there is no separation between home, work, wife, mother, and friend.

My To-Do list is abundant and not exactly in a good way.

Did that last sentence need a comma?

Sigh... I may not know where all the commas go in the land of punctuation (Mrs. Head would not be proud), but I do know that I am using today as a comma.

A break.

A pause.

Separating things I *want* to do and the things I *need* to do.

Today is about the wants, and hopefully it will make all the needs seem a little less needy this week.

Take a moment today to see where you could take a pause from real life and don't worry if you're using it the right way.

There are no rules to life commas. Use as many as you need.

THERE ARE NO RULES TO LIFE COMMAS.

USE AS MANY AS YOU NEED.

LINDA'S TOP TEN

So I needed a little inspiration to get into the writing tonight, and thought to myself... It's Ping's Birthday! We should celebrate the day she was born!

I have my Spotify playlist for The Lucky One playing, because that was one happy memory, and here we go...

- The first time Linda and I met, we were bonding over our extremely sad kindergarten boys who weren't quite ready to go to school all day. We both left our crying children in the classroom, and we cried in the parking lot.

- She can make me laugh with just a look. Usually, that look is saying *WTF?*

- We ~~like~~ love the same books. And movies. And TV shows.

- For a beautiful year, we were both addicted to *Criminal Minds*, to the extent that we could text a quote from a character and know the episode. "Charcoal socks..."

- She once sent me an email with BALLS as the subject line, and for the next two years that became her nickname. Randomly, we would send texts throughout the day with various kinds of balls: tennis, matzo, soccer, and of course, ping-pong. The rest is history.

- We like and dislike the same people.

- She may not agree with me, but I am hoping to be in-laws with her someday.

- She supports everything I do... work (she comes to shows and competitions), writing (I have two followers... and she's both of them), life (she just gets me).

- She answers that call when I just need to tell her about the cute Starbucks guy. *Then,* she goes and gets a coffee just to see him too.

- For my birthday three years ago, she painstakingly printed every post I had ever written on my first blog. A year after that, Blake deleted the blog by mistake, but I still had the majority of my writings. I'm not sure she will ever understand how perfect that gift was, and still is.

I could go on and on, but it would only be inside jokes and complaints. Thank you for being my friend, Ping... I love you like a sister! Hope you had a great day...

THE LIFE LIST

July 18th marked the tenth anniversary of my mother's death, and to honor her memory, I went shopping.

At Target.

Where else would I go? Jacobson's isn't around anymore.

And even though I had told myself I wouldn't buy any books—and only read what I had this summer—I bought a book.

Shocking, I know.

A friend had posted something about it on Facebook, and after reading the blurb, I put it in the cart without a second thought.

It had me at hello.

Or at least it had me from page 5, when the main character, grieving from her mother's death (from ovarian cancer, no less) makes the statement: "I have so much more daughter left in me."

The book is *The Life List* by Lori Nelson Spielman, and in some strange way, it has helped me through this week. I know it seems odd that I would even buy this book, but I am so glad I did, and can't wait for you to read it.

I have been so blessed this summer, reading books that are filled with love, loss, and life, and I can't help but look at my own little book, and wonder if someday we'll be snapping pictures of it on a Target shelf for Instagram.

In a nutshell, books like these make me want to finish my own in hopes of making someone else feel better. I'm not sure it's even about getting it published anymore... that would just be the cherry on top. It's about completion and putting it all out there for the world to see.

It's also about remembering to dream.

In *The Life List* acknowledgments, Lori finishes by writing, *'Finally, this book belongs to every girl and woman who sees the word "dream" and thinks verb, not noun.'*

I think that's a perfect way to end this.

Nine years later, I am reading this again—for the first time—and smiling because Lori is someone I consider a friend. She is the kindest, most generous, and so encouraging to any and all writers. It makes me so happy that I am able to include this today, and able to thank her again for reminding me that dream is a verb. Thank you, Lori!

BOOKS LIKE THESE MAKE ME WANT TO FINISH MY OWN IN HOPES OF MAKING SOMEONE ELSE FEEL BETTER.

AOP

Yesterday I spent a good chunk of time at work going over my AOP (Annual Operating Plan) for 2013. Of course Michael Scofield helped me get through the day, so it wasn't as painful as it sounds.

The time it took me to go over detailed information of this year, break it down, and apply it to 2013 in goals, budget, and numbers was more than I had intended to do. But once I started I couldn't stop.

The more I worked, the more I realized that we should be doing AOPs for our lives, not just work. And by 'we,' I mean 'me.'

But for the sake of this post, let's pretend you want to AOP your own life.

What if we took the time to look over our year—the good, the bad, and the ugly—and try to apply these choices to the next year. I know, I know, it's called 'resolutions' and they have been around forEVER. But how often do you make resolutions based on what you did this year? More often than not, we make a list of things we want to change about ourselves, and poof! There're our New Year's Resolutions. By March, they're forgotten, because most of us really don't want to change that much.

We're a pretty content group, you and I.

I don't force myself into resolutions anymore, mostly because it implies that I'm not good enough the way I am, and I hate that feeling. That feeling is the opposite of enough.

Instead, I'm trying to put my money where my mouth is, and live in the words. For instance, 2012 was about *happiness* and figuring out what that means to me. I think that while it wasn't perfect, it was certainly better than most years. My goal for 2013, as stated in recent posts, is about being present, and I'm definitely curious to see how this will play out. In the next couple days, I'm going to try and find twelve goals to be present and apply each one to a month. I already know yoga and meditation will be there, so wish me luck with that.

I may have to add finishing *Prison Break* to my list as well, since I have to be present while watching that, right?

I'm curious to see if any of you still make resolutions for the year... and how long they last.

I DON'T FORCE
MYSELF INTO
RESOLUTIONS
ANYMORE,
MOSTLY BECAUSE IT
IMPLIES THAT I'M
NOT GOOD ENOUGH
THE WAY I AM,
AND I HATE THAT
FEELING. THAT
FEELING IS THE
OPPOSITE OF
ENOUGH.

THE POWER OF GRATITUDE

Life is really sneaky sometimes.

I seem to recall wanting to learn gratitude in 2013.

Well, be careful what you wish for.

I guess if I were going to wrap up a year about gratitude—and wanted to really drive the point home—losing something as basic as power, and returning it nine *painfully* long days later, would make *anyone* grateful.

Lesson learned.

And perhaps I need to make one final gratitude list for the year as well...

- I am overwhelmingly grateful for our friends who have prayed, listened, hugged, made food, taken our kids in as their own, texted, posted, tweeted, and loved us through it all. I firmly believe that you will see how well you are loved when in crisis. The crisis part is brutal, but we know we are loved. And Twitter makes us giggle.

- I have a whole new respect for Toby, who seems to be able to single-handedly take care of three houses without power. #tobyrules

- Home appliances. You never know how often you use each and every one of them on a daily basis till you can't.

- Clean laundry. I don't think this needs any explanation.

- Home-cooked meals. We have eaten out 99% of our meals these past nine days. Not good for the checking account, nor the waistline.

I know there are more that I will think of later, but I will simply leave you with this picture, which I believe is the epitome of gratitude. It was taken by a friend of mine, and I stole it off her Facebook page. Yes, I asked for permission. Her family (including her parents next door) were out of power for the same amount of time as us, and today she was able to capture so many moments that reflect only love and gratitude... not the anger and frustration of the past nine days. It literally overwhelmed me to tears to look through the picture and see the joy.

So, while I will never want to go through anything like this ever again, it's nice to know that we are surrounded by love and were never alone.

Bless you all who have gotten us through this week. We truly couldn't have done it without you...

Finally, merry and bright...

FLEXIBLE

Flexible: flex·i·ble

adjective 1. capable of bending easily without breaking.

synonyms: pliable, supple, bendable, pliant, plastic;

After the last three weeks, this is the word I have come up with that will be my focus for the year.

Flexible.

For years I have had yoga in the back of my mind. It is just one of those things, like running, that I never thought I could do.

I tried.

I'm really bad.

I woke up really sore.

And I stop.

However, I believe the whole theory behind yoga is to break down that resistant thought pattern, so you can get to the other side. The side that is less rigid, stiff, and uncompromising.

The side that allows more creative thinking.

The side that remembers that everything is going to be okay no matter what.

The side that bends with the ups and downs of life.

The ironic part is you have to let go of everything—all your patterns and stubborn ways—to get to that side, but when you do, it can be more comforting than a bowl of popcorn and binge-watching *Scandal* all night.

Who am I kidding? Nothing is more comforting than popcorn and *Scandal*.

But you know what I mean.

Bottom line is this: I need—*crave*—flexibility in my life. I need to not feel like my body is going to fall apart at any given moment. I need to remember that as a parent, it's not always black and white. I need to bend with the flow of life, and stop breaking with every strong wind (like a tree branch over an electric wire).

Couldn't resist.

So there you have my goal for the year.

I know it comes to you a little later than expected, but maybe I'll be teaching you flexibility as well this year.

What is your word for the year? Make it a good one...

I NEED TO BEND WITH THE FLOW OF LIFE, AND STOP BREAKING WITH EVERY STRONG WIND.

BLAKER'S TOP TEN

This was taken 10 years ago when Blake was one and Evan was five. How can it possibly be that I have an 11 and 15-year-old now? It is shocking what ten years will do!

So in honor of Blake's Birthday, I'd like to do a Top Ten for one of the coolest kids I know.

1. He literally has one of the biggest hearts I know. This kid is thoughtful, kind, and generous. It's not lost on me that he is the most like my mom with his personality.

2. His laughter can be identified in a room of kids.

3. He loves life. Literally, he'll wake up excited, every. single. day.

4. He is loaded with charm and good looks, and he isn't afraid to use them.

5. He loves to write just as much as I do.

6. Any of his problems can be solved with a Slurpee from Speedway.

7. He is tough and fearless. Not always a great combination for a mom to watch over, but it does make the sports more interesting.

8. His medical record includes three concussions, five staples, and twenty stitches in his face. I know he will brag about this someday.

9. His eyes have more expression than his words do sometimes.

10. Kids love him. Parents love him. And pets love him. He is more confident than an 11-year-old should be. I literally can't wait to see what the next year will bring for him!

If any one thing can remind you that life is short, it's baby pictures. There is nothing like going back in time and re-membering how simple life was then. I know we didn't know it at the time, but that's the lesson we must learn.

I will repeat this louder for those in the back:

Life is short.

It will pass you by in a snap if you don't start noticing what is going on now.

Do what you love, and love what you do.

HBD, Blaker.

RELAX

Quick! Raise your hand right now if you are utterly and completely relaxed.

....

Don't worry. I kinda knew no one would run the risk of raising their hand, looking like a ding-dong in front of others. How do I know this? Because none of us are relaxed.

Not a single one.

I'm not sure any of us would know what relaxing was if it hit us in the face. Many of us are given pockets of time, unscheduled—the almighty white-space in our calendars—and we squander it away because we don't want to look like we're not doing something productive. "Productive" is a buzzword that deserves an ass-kicking some days. We have to fill that time with a quick load of laundry or emptying the dishwasher instead of doing something that would make us feel better.

Again, I know this because I have made it my life's quest to fill up the white space. I procrastinate relaxing because I don't want to look like I'm not working hard enough.

What the hell is that about? And who exactly am I trying to impress?

I don't have these answers yet, but I do intend to "research" relaxing today and see what truly is relaxing, and what I think relaxing looks like to others. There's a big difference, and the true benefits of having some downtime will appear when you are using it wisely.

It's Cinco de Mayo today, and I think we could all use a siesta at some point today.

And then a margarita.

I hope you all have a relaxing day.

"PRODUCTIVE" IS A BUZZWORD THAT DESERVES AN ASS-KICKING SOME DAYS.

CLARITY

They say walking is therapy for the soul, and I'm starting to believe them. Who "they" are is a mystery, but I've read it so often lately that I have to give in and jump on board. I just got back from a two-mile walk on the most beautiful morning we've had yet this summer and feel like everything is going to be okay.

Clarity, if you will.

It's the most wonderful feeling after weeks of turmoil, confusion, and loss. Summer does this to me every year, and I have to learn compassion for myself and the others around me. Maybe changing everything about my life isn't the answer I need right now. Maybe learning to accept (and love) what I have at this moment, and know that God will change things when He thinks I need it is what I need right now.

Sometimes the answers are right in front of you too.

Life is so much more than work and making money. Sure, we can't live without them, but at some point we have to make sure that the life we are living is about love rather than obligation. I know I've written about this before, it's a recurring theme in my life, and yet I so easily get off the path every single year. It's as if the fork in the road is taunting me now.

Damn path.

So while I was walking I was making a mental list of things I needed to love my life… and here is what I came up with.

family
friends
writing (and backing it up)
faith

health

books

Half the battle is knowing what you need. Once you can figure that out, the rest is like a rollercoaster ride. Yes, there will be hills, twists and turns that feel far, far away from the path, but soon enough you will find your way back if you stick to what you love.

Work is just that... work. Don't make it your life. And trust that you are exactly where you are supposed to be right now.

Now, head outside and go on a long walk. You'll be glad you did...

AT SOME POINT
WE HAVE TO
MAKE SURE
THAT THE LIFE
WE ARE LIVING
IS ABOUT

Love

RATHER THAN
OBLIGATION.

LETTER TO A NEW MOM

As I sit here tonight it is killing me not to be able to see Sarah and precious little Jonah (Little J-Twizzle, for long). And knowing I was one of the first to even know about him nine months ago, this doesn't seem fair.

I comforted her with the morning sickness.

I sat through nine months of bagel eating.

I hugged and calmed her down when she needed it, right down to the day before.

I tried to be brutally honest with what really happens in delivery so she was prepared.

I told her to get an epidural, even though she was one of those who think they're tough enough.

And I've texted. Oh how I've texted... words of wisdom, dirty jokes, sarcasm, truth, and joy.

To say I make it a priority to help her through life is an understatement, and I don't know what it is that compels me to take on this role, but we are connected in a weird way that cannot be explained.

And if I can't be there this week, there are a few things I want her to know... mom to mom.

First of all, you are going to be overwhelmed. It may not hit today or tomorrow, but it will hit, and when it does you'll wonder why you ever thought being a mother would be cool.

You will fall head over heels in love with this baby, and will find yourself just standing over him to watch him sleep.

Your whole being is going to be taken over by this small, beautiful boy (a boy!!), but you will soon find out that your heart grows even bigger each day. You will have space for Jonah, as well as the life you had before him. Yes, your priorities will change, but it doesn't mean you have to choose one or the other. You will learn the fine art of juggling and relying on your friends... and that's okay.

Postpartum is real. Take it seriously if you're sad.

Ask for and accept help as much as possible, especially at the beginning. You may feel like super-mom (and you are), but none of us got through the first week alone.

Take naps when he naps. Even if it's four to six times a day.

No one cares if your house is a mess.

Be kind to yourself.

Your friends have always been your lifeline. That will not change.

Above all things, remember this: Jonah might be one of the luckiest little boys I know because he has you as his mom. I hope he gets your sense of humor, and especially your snarkiness of late. I hope he follows in your path to be utterly passionate about something when he gets older. I hope he knows he has not just you and Joel, but the entire skating family and the place we call home. You're going to spend hours upon hours worrying about the tiniest issues, but I assure you, everything will be okay in the end.

This should get you through to Friday, when come hell or high water, I'm coming to see Mr. T... with presents and dinner. I plan on holding him for a long time too, so get your fix before I get there.

Until then, you can text me any time day or night.

I can't wait to see how this next part of your life unfolds.

ABOVE ALL THINGS,
REMEMBER THIS:
JONAH MIGHT BE
ONE OF THE
LUCKIEST LITTLE
BOYS I KNOW
BECAUSE HE HAS
YOU AS HIS MOM.

EVAN'S TOP TEN

Sixteen years ago today, at 2:15 in the afternoon, I had my Evan. He was a month early, and is still living life according to Evan.

I cannot believe it's been sixteen years. It's as if time has flown while standing still at times. Every horrible stage felt like it would never end, only to open up to an amazingly wonderful stage. My son would magically appear, new and improved. Oh, Dr. Spates had warned me that kids would also regress right before a growth spurt, mentally and physically.

And boy, was she right.

So, of course in my own fashion, I'd like to take a moment and remember the wonderful stages...

1. He is funny. I married funny, and had a funny son. Funny how that works out.

2. He loves every. single. animal. on the planet. But mostly he loves his Goldie Girl. The two of them are like two peas in a pod. Their favorite game to this day is hide-and-seek. If you've never seen a boy play hide and seek with a dog, you're missing out.

3. He's smart. He doesn't always know this, and quickly forgets when he does, but I know it's in there.

4. He is a genuinely nice person. It astounds me how much he cares about other people.

5. He is friends with everyone. He doesn't want anyone to feel left out, and truly tries to be nice to most people.

6. He spends a great deal of time trying to figure out a way to scare me. He'll hide around corners, in closets, and behind doors in order to do this. It's not my favorite thing about him, but still I wouldn't want him to stop any time soon either.

7. He has grown to be really grateful and thankful. It's no secret that the past few years have been much tougher than usual, and he never complains. Well, almost never.

8. His hair. Yes, it's long, and at one time looked a little like Bieber, but now it's just him. To love Evan is to love his hair... give it time, it'll grow on you.

9. He can do spot-on imitations of many people... mostly those with a lisp. Now looking back at #4, all I can say is he'd never do this in front of them. His voices are the best.

10. Even though he tells Blake that he's adopted on a daily basis, he's still a good big brother. Last night during Mass while saying the Our Father, he squeezed Blake's hand so hard he yelped and doubled over. The row in front of us started to laugh with us. I know it's not appropriate, but those are the moments they will remember. He is teaching him to be a better person in many little ways, and even if he doesn't know it, Blake adores him. I can't wait to see them ten years from now.

And no I'm not wishing the time away... just looking forward to a fun future.

HBD Ev!

HE IS TEACHING
HIM TO BE A
BETTER PERSON IN
MANY LITTLE WAYS,
AND EVEN IF HE
DOESN'T KNOW IT,
Blake adores him.

UNFINISHED

I imagine the last tenth of a mile in a marathon feels like the last two weeks of school. When you're running a marathon (again, I can only imagine), hitting the twenty-six-mile mark must feel like the end, and that the last point-two were created by someone with a serious mean streak in them.

That's exactly what kids think of the last two weeks of school. Everyone is done with homework, assignments, papers, and tests. They have worked hard all year, completed what the teachers gave them, and now that Spring is officially here, they couldn't care less where the finish line is. But there's still the issue of two weeks left.

And it's kinda how I feel about finishing anything in life. Somewhere along the line I have become the world's greatest starter of all things.

I can start books I'll never finish reading.

I can start projects that will never get done. (I secretly believe this is why God created Pinterest).

I can start diets and 'healthy life changes' only to be sore, hungry, and pissed off.

And the Mother of all things unfinished... I can start writing projects that are avoided when the going gets tough.

Procrastination is my middle name, and *I have no time* is my mantra.

It's no secret that A.A. Milne is probably my most favorite for the best quotes ever, but this one takes the cake. It's almost as if one of my friends made this quote up and pasted his name on it just so I would find it... on Pinterest... while not writing that next scene.

"So perhaps the best thing to do is to stop writing Introductions and get on with the book."

— A.A. Milne

I have a vague recollection of things that I have finished...
- ✓ Ratings
- ✓ Various 5Ks and walking a marathon
- ✓ My first book

...and the thing that I remember the most about any of these accomplishments is having the most amazing feeling of pride when it was all said and done. It was a feeling that I could do or be anything I wanted, and it was all true. I think if I could bottle up that feeling, I would make millions. Most of us walk around with a slight feeling of inadequacy—a symptom of motherhood—and I think life would be so much better if we could see all the good we do, all the time. The daily stuff is finished sometimes without even thinking. Making lunches... getting kids to school on time (or early like today)... getting stuff done at work... making dinner when there's nothing in the house.... sitting through endless games… balancing the checkbook. These are all things we finish every day and don't even realize that out there, somewhere, some people don't do this stuff. Every mom I know goes above and beyond what is expected.

In the Land of Motherhood, we are the finishers. When it comes to our own lives, we need some work. Some will argue that once you become a mother you give up your own life, and I will kindly disagree. I think when you give up on your hopes and dreams, a little thing called 'resentment' creeps into your life, and makes for a really cranky mom. Take a moment and see if you know a mom like that... one who appears to be super-mom, but you know she is seething on the inside.

A marathon is finished one step at a time.

A school year is completed one class at a time.

And a book is written one word—one letter—at a time.

None of it has to be perfect, but I think it's important to have something to work towards other than the next lacrosse game. It could be cooking or photography. Reading or even blogging.

Take a moment this long weekend to check in and see if there is something missing in your life, and how you can start filling the gap.

And then take that first step...

I think life would be so much better if we could see all the good we do, all the time.

FIVE CENTS FOR HELP

I have had one of those weeks when I began to question why I dropped out of Psych 101 all those years ago. It seemed as though everyone was going through something, and my job was to help them. And now that I really think about it, my life is kinda like that. I feel as though my job description should include counselor or mentor… something along those lines.

Life coach, anyone?

Don't get me wrong, I'm not complaining at all. In fact, truth be told, I get a little giddy when I get to listen and help someone work through a problem. It has occurred to me on more than one occasion that this is the reason I am here. I love being able to laugh with someone or cry with them too. I love to see the lightbulb go off when they see the answer for themselves. I love the hugs that follow… or sometimes chocolate.

Chocolate is always good.

I have often wondered why I have chosen to write about the words, but now I get it. It's my way of conducting mass therapy for all. I simply want us all to have a better life.

To make better choices.

To see the bright side.

To make the change that is long overdue.

To be grateful and say thank you.

To know that happiness isn't something you have to look for.

To understand that letting go is okay.

To find your path.

I was recently asked to write something for someone who has been a part of my life for the past nineteen years (maybe more, and yes, it's been that long). She is finally taking the plunge and doing something she has wanted to do for a long time, and while that can be exciting, it's also a little scary. The words 'Be careful what you wish for' resonate in times like this. I have no doubt she is doing exactly what she is supposed to be doing, otherwise the stars wouldn't have lined up for her this way. But just the same, change can be hard.

I have given this so much thought, because you know I want to get it right. The last thing she needs is a lame post about following your dreams, blah, blah, blah. Then I realized, almost every post I write is for her. When I sit down to do this, I am usually carrying around what is going on in my life, or in my friends' lives, and I write for them. I try to inspire, encourage, and problem solve along the way, and if something makes you giggle, well then my job is done.

And sometimes I need to borrow from others to convey precisely what I want to say...

"More than anything, I know that you just have to choose to make the best of things. You get one life, and it only goes forward. And there really are all kinds of happy endings."
— Katherine Center

I think she'd approve.

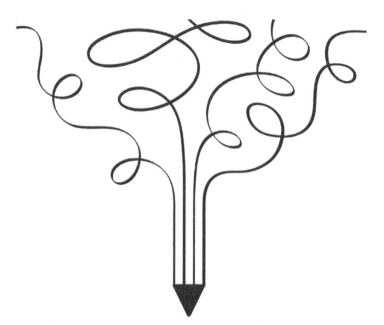

WHEN I SIT DOWN TO
DO THIS, I AM USUALLY
CARRYING AROUND
WHAT IS GOING ON IN
MY LIFE, OR IN MY
FRIENDS' LIVES,

and I write for them.

OVERHEATED

It's no secret I have a love/hate relationship with Bikram Yoga. Everyone who practices says you have to give it time... Five classes, they say, is the magic number when you stop wishing you were in an igloo the entire time you're in there.

Well, I'm here to tell you that if I were to base it on my fifth class, I probably wouldn't go back.

It was hell.

Literally.

And crowded. And long. And I wanted anything other than to be there.

After the class, I sat on the bench outside the studio, blinking back tears, while the teacher tried to talk me off the ledge. It only made me want to cry more. As someone who prides herself on being strong, to feel this defeated over yoga was pretty humbling.

That was the hate part.

A few days later I didn't have time to go in, so I just did a yoga video at home. It was then and there that I realized yoga had invaded my brain, and I would probably never do anything again without focusing intensely on my breath.

I finished the video with a new outlook about the five classes I had accomplished (and for anyone who has ever done even one class, you understand the meaning of accomplishment with new eyes). The video is hard, but certainly nothing like what I had been through in the past couple weeks. When I was done, I realized that I had gained much more than physical strength during those 450 minutes of yoga: I was mentally stronger than I was two weeks ago, and that's saying a lot after ten months of winter.

I thought I'd share with you a few things Bikram Yoga has taught me:

- I am stronger than I think. This class will break you down in the first ten minutes if you don't continually tell yourself that you just need to get through the next exercise. And then the next one...

- Being perfect at something... *anything* is just an illusion. Don't get me wrong—I don't think I'm perfect at *anything*, but I tend to stay in the safe zone when it comes to working out (and life). Walking, running, elliptical... nothing that is going to push me in any way. And having spent the majority of my life on skates, that really isn't a challenge either. It's good for me to fail miserably at something like I did in my fifth class.

- We can pretty much get through anything, one breath at a time. This practice should be mandatory for women considering getting pregnant.

- Focusing on one point is the single greatest skill you can acquire to learn balance. Right now I'm focusing on a glass of wine. Life is about balance, and that is sometimes found in a glass. No judging.

- I don't give up easily. Even though I usually think of myself as the queen of starting things, I am learning to finish things too. I don't like letting myself down, and have figured out what things are really important to me. Those are the things I'm finishing. I'm a finisher.

I know that I have easily sweated out my body weight in the last two weeks, and I also know that I will go back again and again. In a year that is about flexibility, I am learning so much more... but I guess that was the point all along.

BEING PERFECT
AT SOMETHING...
anything
IS JUST
AN ILLUSION.

MEET GRACIE

You're standing at the top of a bridge, harnessed in, attached to a bungee rope. The wind is whipping, and your knees are shaking. You can feel your stomach near your heart, which by the way, is beating madly. Your eyes water as you hear your friends cheering you on. Everything in your body says no, but there's that tiny little voice that says... *yes*.

Can you feel it?

And when you're done you can't wipe the smile off your face. You did something crazy and incredible, and now you carry that memory with you for the rest of your life.

How often does this happen in our lives?

Probably once if we're lucky, but more often than not, it's never.

And that's okay, really. I'm not here to make you feel bad that you don't have million-dollar dreams and goals that are unattainable.

But as I was working on my next project, I did realize that the advice one of my characters is giving might be beneficial to you as well. I know most of us are still just going through the days, trying to get to the next one, or the next weekend. Always something to look forward to, but never focused on the now. It's time to start living, and giving our own lives the attention they deserve.

Gracie's Steps to Reinvention

- Take care of your health. This is non-negotiable.

- Find your hobby. Not a job. Not a kid. Something that you can lose yourself in even for a small amount of time each day.

- Take 24 hours before making any decisions. Any. Decision. At. All.

- Journal every day. Have a place to dump all the thoughts that you can't say out loud. It doesn't have to be long or well written. Just get the thoughts out of your head.

- Have a connection... a touchstone, a theme song, a prayer that will bring you back to this place of knowing what is most important to you.

No, these are life changing ideas, and they seem so simple, but how many of us are doing these every day? I would love to tell a coworker that I needed to check with someone before taking their Sunday morning shift. My initial instinct is always to make someone else feel better, even at my own expense.

~~Sometimes~~ Always, I regret this quick decision.

Life is a work in progress, a journey, and it's not meant to be mastered by the age of forty.

I actually think that's when life really begins.

So take a moment today and think about what you could (reasonably) change in your life to make it better? Is there a hobby calling your name... photography, maybe? Can you fit in a walk, even if it's a short one? What song would be playing if you were walking down a runway?

Today is about inspiring yourself. Take the time to do one thing on the list today... two, if you're feeling adventurous. Start somewhere, anywhere, and see how it makes you feel.

LIFE IS A WORK IN PROGRESS, A JOURNEY, AND IT'S NOT MEANT TO BE MASTERED BY THE AGE OF FORTY. I ACTUALLY THINK THAT'S WHEN LIFE REALLY BEGINS.

FABULOUS

Years ago, there was a book called *The Book of Awesome*, featuring the most mundane things as awesome (buttered toast, towels just out of the dryer, etc...) and I loved it. It was one of those be-grateful-for-the-ordinary books that really hit the nail on the head. When you're grateful for what you already have, life becomes... Well, awesome.

It was fabulous.

And today, when I was walking, I started to think about it. After two walks this week that left me wondering when I got so out of shape, today was sweltering, sweaty, energizing, and fabulous. It was a walk that gave me hope that maybe I wasn't so... well, hopeless. By the end of the walk I was thinking of spinning again. That's how good the walk was.

I also started to wonder what else I could do, what other walls I could push through, to get to the other side where fabulous waits, and immediately writing came to mind. It's so similar to working out it scares me.

It's always something I feel like I have to do, but AL-WAYS feel better when I'm done.

It's one of those few things in life that leaves me with more energy and excitement.

It produces hope and joy... two things I can never have enough of.

Here are a few other things that I think are just fabulous...

That perfect margarita on a hot summer night.

The text that comes at *exactly* the moment you need it.

The power nap.

Hearing laughter from your kids.

Songs that make you want to dance.

Dancing.

Action films featuring Channing Tatum.

Iced coffee.

Reading through old posts and having the strongest feeling of wonder and pride.

Planning a girls weekend.

The gift of writing.

Of course I could go on and on, because life is fabulous. Sometimes we just have to recognize it, accept it into our lives, and let go of the stuff that brings us down. I read a passage in a book recently that put it as simply as this: Do you want to be happy, or do you want to hang on to the baggage of the past?

I know, more than anyone else, that while it seems like an easy choice, it's not always that easy. I am working on letting go, and I hope you are too.

What's on your fabulous list? Yes, you have to write one now.

SOMETIMES WE
JUST HAVE TO
RECOGNIZE IT,
ACCEPT IT INTO
OUR LIVES, AND
LET GO OF

**THE
STUFF
THAT
BRINGS US
DOWN**

TO-BE

Sometimes I wonder if this is the lifelong quest for all of us. What if our job, our only job, was to figure out what made us happy, and we did it like we were getting paid?

What if you got paid to do something that made you happy?

Not your spouse.

Not your kids.

Not your boss.

Not even the damn dog.

And what if what made you happy didn't make anyone else happy in your family? Would you still do it? With gusto? I believe this is the missing link. We look for what we want, daydream about doing it, and maybe even try something new. But the *second* it feels uncomfortable—or we couldn't do the twenty other things on our To-Do list—we throw in the towel and think it was just a silly pipe dream.

I saw a picture on Instagram today and it stopped me from flipping through any other pictures. Someone had taken a picture of their To-Do list, only it filled just one side of the page. On the other side, she had her **To-Be** list, and it was filled with things like grateful, vulnerable, curious, and generous. What if you started your day wanting to be courageous or daring? Or frivolous or light?

We stop ourselves so often, every single day really, because it's more comfortable to just keep doing what we know.

Safe.

I don't think the word "safe" would ever be on a To-Be list.

It's a given we can't get rid of our To-Do list altogether, but maybe adding one To-Be at the top of the page is more doable for you. Baby steps. That's how we make any changes in life.

What will be on your To-Be list tomorrow?

And yes, I expect you to do this.

_____

_____

_____

_____

_____

_____

_____

_____

_____

_____

_____

_____

_____

_____

_____

_____

_____

_____

_____

WHAT IF OUR JOB,
OUR ONLY JOB,
WAS TO FIGURE
OUT WHAT MADE
US HAPPY, AND
WE DID IT LIKE
WE WERE
GETTING PAID?

A DAY IN THE LIFE

Have you ever noticed when you decide to make a momentous change, life has a way of trying to push you back into your old ways?

You start a diet, and a coworker brings in brownies.

You vow to spend less money, and there's a sale at Target.

You promise to forgive and forget, and you're faced with issues you didn't even know you had!

It's the boomerang effect. And now that you know it exists, it should make it easier to plan for it. Let's face it, God has a sense of humor, and I think He's testing to see if we're serious with the choices we make.

For instance, here is a list of things that happened just yesterday... keep in mind I'm trying to keep the past in the past and forgive myself or anyone else.

9:00 am: Get to work and everything is hunky-dory.

9:15 am: I never did a Regional Number sign up. The coaches have to send out last-minute emails to their parents, reminding them that it starts at 4 p.m.... that same day.

11:00 am: UPS guy shows up *without* my rushed order for a boy's basic skills costume. Apparently, I didn't know he was a boy when I ordered him a girl's costume. Nice.

Noon: I realize I'm the worst friend possible and forgot to wish Linda a happy birthday. Ping!

1:15 pm: While setting out the costumes, I realized that I ordered the learn-to-skate boys' pants but no shirts. I never order pants, and *only* order shirts for the show. This should be interesting.

5:20 pm: I realize that I also forgot to order skirts for one of our other numbers. They have leotards, but no skirts. Happens to be the same group with vocal parents. They are kind, but make no mistake, I'll have to fix this today. And for the tenth time, I **KNOW** they want hot-pant shorts instead of skirts.

I. Get. It.

9:30 pm: Yes, I'm still at the rink and trying to close the registers. Something goes wrong, and I can't for the life of me figure out why only the concession register is showing up on the report. I can hear a coworker in my head saying *"What the hell?"* and I begin to beat myself up.

10:00 pm: I get home, crack a beer, and cry.

I was able to get through the entire day until that point. Sure, I was frustrated at times, but everyone around me was able to sympathize or at least understand. But for some reason, closing did me in.

I went to bed and really thought about the day. Sure it had been hell, but I handled it. The only thing that was really bothering me was closing, and it dawned on me—closing is not my thing! Numbers are not my thing. And, while I so desperately wanted to do a good job, I at least did the best I could. I'm not going to be that person that 'does' everything well. I am good at a lot of things, but I need to remember my limitations, and forgive them too.

Today, the sun is shining. I don't have to work until tonight, and I am writing. All is well. I called Debbie last night and told her she may have a puzzle this morning, so I am just going to do my best not to worry about what I did, or what they'll say. I know it'll bug me for a bit, but I will do my best to let it go.

Thanks for the wakeup call, God. Maybe next time it doesn't have to happen all in one day, and for the record, I'm not giving up.

I AM GOOD AT A
LOT OF THINGS,
BUT I NEED TO
REMEMBER MY
LIMITATIONS,
AND FORGIVE
THEM TOO.

ENDINGS AND BEGINNINGS

*"All endings are also beginnings.
We just don't know it at the time."*

— Mitch Albom

So, yesterday was my last shift ever at the rink, and it's just hitting me now that it was the last weekend I'll have to work. The last shift I'll have to dread. The last time I'll have to answer the same endless questions.

I know there will be other endless questions in my future, but we have a couple years for that.

For now, I am surprisingly content with the feeding-diaper-playtime cycle I have every three hours. It actually feels like I have my life back for the first time in a long time.

Too long, if you ask me.

The past two months have been a whirlwind of changes. Changes for my kids, for me, for seasons, and for my family. Some are good changes, and some are a little more difficult, but since I am here to find the #dailyinspiration in life, we are going to find the good in all of this.

The biggest thing I've learned in the past two months is that more than anything, I need to write for myself again. I spent a lot of time last year trying to figure out what anyone needed to hear. Writing for an audience is the quickest way for me to procrastinate. I will clean out junk drawers, do five loads of laundry, and bake a batch of cookies before I could figure out what to write to you. Yes, I've done all of that today.

The best thing you can do is stop worrying about what everyone else expects from you. Do your best in whatever comes your way and use your own judgment. If something makes you happy, keep at it. If not, find a plan B, C, or D. Don't ever forget there are twenty-six letters in the alphabet.

Which leads me to the next thing I've learned about change: There are no rules. Nothing in this world is permanent, and you can start over at any time. Sometimes, we are forced to start over, but hopefully you have some choice in the matter. Either way, make up your own rules as you go. Don't let anyone tell you how to do something, because nothing else matters other than how you feel or what you want. Always trust your gut, even if it's telling you to nanny triplets.

Lastly, take your time. Good things take time, and by forcing or rushing change, you're just making it more difficult to see clearly. If something doesn't work out, then it wasn't meant to be... trust me on this. It has taken me years to get to this point where I feel like stars are actually lining up for me. I'm not feeling that anxiety that says things like, "When this week is over, I'll relax." Anxiety is a bitch and will always make you feel bad.

I left my anxiety in the left bottom drawer... the one with the candy.

And the Baileys.

I also know that *life is life* and won't always be rainbows and butterflies. But, for the time—and a long time coming—I am happy with the changes... even the hard ones.

Are you ready for a change?

There are no rules.

**NOTHING IN
THIS WORLD IS
PERMANENT,
AND YOU CAN
START OVER
AT ANY TIME.**

WANTS

There are many things I am pretty good at, but there is one thing in this world that I am exceptional at, and that's giving advice. I'm not always good at *taking* advice, and certainly not my own, but that's one of the things I'm going to start working on.

Yes, I can talk the talk, but walking it is entirely different, and often find myself tripping and falling. Tonight's topic came to me after I gave advice to someone who is nervous about the next two weeks. "Handle one moment at a time and don't ask any more than that of yourself," I told her.

If only I could whisper this to myself every now and again, I might start sleeping better.

I know with the drama and deadlines of our lives, it's hard to keep perspective. It's almost impossible to keep focus on what is most important when bills are due, we're running late, we've failed a test, or when people around us just suck the happy out of the room.

And when we somehow do get through that moment, another one comes along to stray us away from what is important. It's an uphill battle, but I think that's the lesson; Do we want our lives to be about the drama or what's important to us?

I know what I want, and I know what you probably want too. It's not hard to see when it's written here in black and white. The challenge is living in the moment every single day, and not taking anything for granted. Good, bad, or ugly, things happen to us, and our challenge is to make our life better because of those moments.

Are you up to that challenge?

How are you going to choose to spend the moments of your life?

Raise your hand if you—like me—are always on a mission to improve your life in some way.

Starting a diet?

Buying new planners or systems?

Books that promise the perfect morning routine that will change your life?

Bad-assery?

You can put your hand down now. I had mine up for all of them.

I have spent half of my life searching for someone else to tell me how to live my life, and the one thing I've learned is that the only expert we will ever need is ourselves.

We can be the experts of our own lives if we could just begin to listen to what we really need.

I've spent the last few days feeling as lost and scared as everyone else about the state of the world we're living in. The answers we're seeking right now aren't going to be found in a book. We're certainly not going to find it on the news. Netflix is a lovely escape, but even that can feel monotonous by day six.

Nope, the only way you're going to get through this and maintain any level of sanity is by knowing what is good for you. What works. And, more importantly, what doesn't.

Sometimes, the best way to figure out what we DO want is to simply be clear about what we DON'T want. We're stuck at home, but that doesn't mean it has to feel like a prison.

Learn something new.

Crochet a scarf.

Start that journal you've been thinking about.

Create a blog.

Zoom or FaceTime with friends.

Download a book.

Scrapbook or start a recipe book of your own.

Make a 2020 Playlist and have some fun with it.

Pray a Hail Mary or better yet, learn to say the Rosary.

Harry Potter marathon? Anyone?

Look, I know the times are tough and scary, but taking care of ourselves is essential before we can take care of anyone else. Turn the news off and go for a socially-distant walk outside. Take a nap. Drive through Starbucks and pay for the person behind you.

Apparently, baking bread is a thing now, too.

You get the picture. Be curious and open to what makes you happy. The operative word there was happy.

We will get through this, and we will be stronger people when this is all said and done.

And hopefully, you learn a little something about yourself you didn't know before. It's why we're here.

Be safe. Wash your hands. Love one another. Be kind.

I HAVE SPENT
HALF OF MY LIFE
SEARCHING FOR
SOMEONE ELSE
TO TELL ME HOW
TO LIVE MY LIFE,
AND THE ONE
THING I'VE
LEARNED IS
THAT THE ONLY
EXPERT WE WILL
EVER NEED IS
ourselves.

ESSENTIAL

Essential: Adj: *absolutely necessary; extremely important.*
Noun: *a thing that is absolutely necessary.*
How many weeks has this been? Is it still April? The days are blending into one another, much like my thoughts, and don't even get me started on how much I've spent on groceries. No one in this house can stop eating, myself included. Having a home office located in our kitchen isn't exactly ideal for me.

I get it. Some of us quarantine better than others—that's a given—but all of us are starting to feel the walls closing in. Especially here in dreary Michigan, where a sunny day is as rare as a unicorn.

Or is it?

As I write this, sunlight is streaming through our front windows with blinding strength. The kind of bright that makes you want to wear sunglasses indoors. The kind of sunlight that is whispering something to me.

Dream, it says.

Dream of a better day ahead of you.

Think of what you want to do first when this quarantine has lifted. I know the world is going to look different, but what from your pre-quarantine life is essential to you?

For me, it's getting together with friends. The Friday happy hour or Sunday Funday. Being able to give a friend a random hug. Working in an office.

Shopping at Target without a mask.

I know, these things sound frivolous when people are fighting for their lives with this virus. Or you're one of the brave souls who put on your work clothes and head into the hospital every day. I know your wishes are far different than mine, and that's okay. We all have a different take on this pandemic and will struggle/deal with it in our own way.

There are no instructions on how to quarantine properly. No pandemic guidebook to ease your worries. We have a few more weeks of this and need to keep our eyes on the future and our hearts in the here and now. Be kinder to yourself and those around you, every day, and remember this isn't something we've ever been through. There are no right or wrong answers.

So, for today, I want you to take in the sunshine and the warmer temperature—wherever you are—and trust that you are exactly where you need to be. We will get through this with more awareness of ourselves, and create more understanding and a grateful world in the future.

And when in doubt, read something wonderful.

DREAM OF A BETTER DAY AHEAD OF YOU.

HOW CAN I HELP?

I recently ran out of things to watch on Netflix, so I began to watch *New Amsterdam* on demand. Have you seen this show? Yes, I know, the last thing TV needs is another hospital drama, but I'm telling you, this show will make you feel good. Sappy, laughter-through-tears good. Its specialty is highlighting how amazing doctors and nurses are—any hospital staff, really—and that's something we should all embrace right now.

And, even though it's fiction, I can't help but get sucked in by every episode, resulting in happy tears in the final moments of each episode.

It's a show about hope.

It's a show about love.

It's a show that reinforces being a good human above all else.

And it's a show you need to watch if you just want to feel better.

"How can I help?" This line is said about ten times in the first episode alone by the main character, Max Goodwin. It's brilliant.

I just started episode four, and he said it again. Instantly, I knew this is what I would write about this week.

These times are tough on all of us. Social distancing and lockdowns have become the new normal, but is it really? This feels anything but normal. And does anyone else feel like the phrase social distancing is an oxymoron? As much as I hate to say this, I think we're going to be here for a while.

So my question is this: How can I help?

I have made it a mission on my Facebook page to try and bring a smile or laughter to your day. At least five times every day, I feel like breaking down. And I'm betting I'm not alone in feeling this way. I turn to social media to find something—anything—to feel better or laugh about. So, my goal during this crazy time right now is to find something that brings me joy. Then I try to bring you joy. I obsessively use my Calm app. I bake like I'm a contestant on a baking show. A daily adventure involves getting a McDonald's Diet Coke. Don't judge.

And I watch shows like *New Amsterdam*.

Our lives are filled with enough reality. Letting go of what you believe "normal" is supposed to look like will help you get through this period of time. You'll need to find a way to manage your moods like it was your job.

Because it is.

We need you, heart and soul. We need you to be able to laugh through the tears. And on those days that feel pretty dark, let me leave this one question here for you...

How can I help?

WE NEED YOU, HEART
AND SOUL. WE NEED
YOU TO BE ABLE TO
LAUGH THROUGH THE
TEARS. AND ON THOSE
DAYS THAT FEEL
PRETTY DARK, LET ME
LEAVE THIS ONE
QUESTION HERE FOR
YOU...

How can I help?

HOME STRETCH

Home stretch: The final part of a racecourse from the last curve to the finish line. The final part of a distance or the final effort needed to finish. *I think we're finally on the home stretch with this project.*

I bet you all didn't know that my dad is a HUGE horse racing fan. Like, not just the Kentucky Derby interest, but pretty much any horse race that's on, kind of commitment. On Saturday night we watched the replay of the 2015 Preakness Stakes.

Now, *that's* a commitment.

It was so long ago, I think he was still surprised by the winner (American Pharoah, if you're wondering). And the funny part is, I had to change it from regular horse racing to watch a replay of an old horse race. Apparently, horse racing is the ONLY current sport right now, and it's on every single weekend.

You may have gotten the snapchats.

Horses are beautiful, and the sport of horse racing is very exciting. I'm not downplaying any of that, but having to watch it every weekend is beginning to take a toll. I've started taking my Kindle and happily reading while we're off to the races. I'm obsessed with Words with Friends again. I've also been known to take a power nap while the races are on.

To be completely honest, without the crowd, the races are a little boring. Watching the difference of the before and after, I began to wonder, what will our after look like? How different is our new normal going to look once the quarantine is lifted?

While watching the 2015 version, I literally cringed as I watched the crowd and HOW CLOSE everyone was to each other. I think I'll be forever changed by this, and I still don't know how to process that, let alone label it as good or bad. If I'm being completely honest, I'm a little nervous about the future. I think it's going to be a very different world we live in.

That being said, there are things that only a quarantine can force someone to learn. For instance, training a puppy is simultaneously as easy and as hard as it sounds. Not much better than a newborn at times, but just like a newborn, the joy far outweighs the drama.

Cooking has also become even more of a hobby these days. I'm no longer content with the same old meals and have tried to make some new things during this time.

I've finally perfected my chocolate chip cookie recipe and make them more than I care to admit.

I'm writing every day, and loving the direction of book four.

Hulu is my new best friend.

My Calm app is still my daily companion.

And I'm grateful. Grateful for all the little things I see now that I didn't when I was racing around in 'real life.' Music, flowers, birds, and the ping of a text from a friend. I appreciate my friends so much more now.

Yoga pants.

So for today, knowing we're in the home stretch, I want to know what you're grateful for during this time. It's so easy to watch the news and complain, but I challenge you to find a different perspective. I want you to look around and appreciate exactly where you are right now. And if you can't, then what is it you'd change? It's okay to visit Pity City, but it's not okay to live there.

Find something to be grateful for as if it were your job.

Because it is.

And then read something fabulous. Because you've earned it.

CHOOSING JOY

*"They say a person needs just three things to be truly happy
in this world: someone to love, something to do,
and something to hope for."*
— Tom Bodett

So, I'll just state the obvious… This last week has been another shining example of everything that's wrong with the world. This isn't a political post by any means, and I'm certainly not going to throw another opinion in the mix. We don't need any more rants or protests in the world, and here's the deal… I'm not going to tell you what you *do* need. That is not my job. The only thing I can do is continue to try and figure out what it is that I need to live in this world. It's a daily battle, and I don't always win.

But that's okay because my lessons will continue to show up in one form or another until I finally learn.

Choosing joy isn't exactly new to me. I've written about it. I've posted about it. I've rallied for it. And yet, at the end of ten weeks of quarantine, I'm feeling the need to search for it again. I genuinely believe the answers we are searching for is finding out what makes us happy. And this isn't a one-size-fits-all answer. Nor is the mission ever complete. What made me happy in my twenties is far different from what makes me happy now.

Hell, what made me happy ten weeks ago looks different than it does now.

I don't know what June will bring, but I do know that the world is different now, and it's our J O B to continue to grow with it. It's your choice—always has been—to find your joy.

You have to let go of the stuff you don't want in order to make room for the stuff you do. You can't have both.

You can't have resentment and be grateful.

You can't be self-sacrificing and fulfilled.

You can't be everything to everyone without losing a part of yourself.

You have to choose yourself first. I don't know how I wrote an entire book about this last year and it's just now hitting me how much those words resonate with me.

I see that now.

Gratitude and happiness are choices—daily battles, sometimes—and always based on your own perspective. Sure, there are horrible things in the world, but only we can choose where our focus lies.

Homework: Your mission, should you choose to accept it, is to find ONE thing that brings you joy every day. Of course, you can do more (make a list!), but starting small with just one thing will begin a shift into something bigger. It's not a contest, and only you can decide what your one thing is. I'm going to post mine on Instagram and try to have some fun with it.

I hope you do the same.

And when in doubt, find something fabulous to read. :)

YOU HAVE TO
LET GO OF
THE STUFF YOU
DON'T WANT
IN ORDER TO
MAKE ROOM FOR
**THE STUFF
YOU DO.**
YOU CAN'T HAVE BOTH.

OFFENSE VS. DEFENSE

If you are a human, chances are you have had a chance to witness a game between two teams at some point in your life. Perhaps your kids are in team sports.

Maybe you are.

I'm going to use hockey in our post today because that is what I know. In my heart, in my bones, I know hockey. I know what is needed to be a great player, and even more importantly, a great team member. I have coached hockey players. Raised a hockey player. Worked with hockey players.

I know the mentality and respect it.

And, I'm willing to go out on a limb when I say that most of what applies with hockey can transfer over to other sports... at least the big picture ideas I'm talking about today.

The offense vs. defense theory.

In one of Blake's first years of hockey, he was on a team that lost almost every game. I think they won two out of fifty-plus games. It wasn't pretty, and most of us chalked it up to a character-building year. What else can you do in that situation?

About halfway through the season, I began to pinpoint where the wheels fell off, and the idea of what happened with that team never left me. The biggest problem (in my humble opinion) was the fact that our goaltending wasn't the strongest. Look, I know, they're kids, and yes I believe everyone was doing their best. I'm certainly not goalie-bashing. Stick with me here.

If you're on a team with a weaker goalie, then what happens is the rest of the team begins to play defense. You lose your offense—and with it, your main ability to score—and everyone is playing solely to not get scored on. If you're playing like this, it's hard to see, because you're so busy defending your zone.

You guys, this is life.

You are either living defensively—protecting what's yours—or you are living offensively and seeking creative ways to solve your problems. Curious and open to trying new things. Let's pretend we all have a goalie in our lives who's let a few soft goals in. It happens.

You gained a few pounds.

You stopped taking care of yourself.

You're in a rut of work, eat, sleep, repeat.

You begin to notice that you complain about E V E R Y T H I N G. Everything.

Every day, you set out and try your hardest not to screw anything up. Keep things the way they are… don't rock the boat. And for God's sake, don't step outside your comfort zone.

This is living defensively, and I hate to blame an entire year, but 2020 has given many of us this defensive perspective. The why-bother attitude with a side of *what difference does it make?*

I'm here to tell you that your mental state does make a difference. Waking up and saying "why not?" instead of "why bother?" is a day-maker. Replacing the phrase "have to" with "get to" is another trick for your mind.

I have to go to work today.

I get to go to work today.

See the difference? The second choice feels almost grateful for the ability to have a job at all.

Is this year everything we thought it would be? Definitely not, but that doesn't mean we can't turn it around ourselves. We can, and it's your responsibility to make those changes. No one else is going to do it for you. Take ownership of your life—be your own coach—and see where you need to make changes to live life playing offense. The only thing we ever have control over is our own perspective and how we choose to see the world around us.

Choose wisely, my friends.

Go team!

Until next time, read something fabulous…

THE ONLY THING
WE EVER HAVE
CONTROL OVER IS
*OUR OWN
PERSPECTIVE*
AND HOW WE
CHOOSE TO SEE
THE WORLD
AROUND US.

2020 VISION

I don't have twenty-twenty vision. In fact, I'm blind as a bat, and even with glasses, it'll never be twenty-twenty. I've learned to get along with what I have, making the most of it and being happy it doesn't change too much from year to year.

This year—like my eyesight—has been anything but normal for what we envisioned back in January. Raise your hand if you started the year off thinking it was going to be just another year. Or maybe you had big plans to get married, or graduate, or start a new job. Chances are, you still did some of those things, but I know it turned out far different than when you first imagined it. My old coaching motto—*the reality doesn't fit the image*—explains a lot about the year 2020.

The thing is, every one of us—no matter what your eyesight is like—has a case of 2020 vision. It is impossible to have gone through this year and still see life the same way you did way back in 2019. The never-ending disappointments, cancellation of life events, the job loss, the isolation, the illness, and the massive loss of so many loved ones.

Not to mention the constant confusion of what's real, what's fake, and who you can trust. We have been pushed to the very brink of our own sanity, and what do we have to show for it? For some, it's a new hobby, and for others it might be a few extra pounds. Some enjoyed the challenge of puzzles, and others got a puppy. Some found solace in at-home workouts, while others binged on every episode of *West Wing, Schitt's Creek,* and *The Great British Bake Off.*

Remember, this is a no-judgment zone…

One lesson we learned was there isn't a guidebook to social distancing or how to quarantine properly. When life threw lemons at us, we had to figure out our own special recipe for lemonade. From what I've seen—even with my faulty, limited eyesight—this year gave us more hardship than we ever thought possible, but I've also seen things like compassion, generosity, and growth. I guarantee we have all changed and are better humans because of this year. We simply can't go through a year like this unaffected. Again… it's impossible.

December always makes me hopeful for the upcoming year. I love a fresh start, a new calendar, and a fresh perspective, but it's always good to look back to see what we know now that we didn't twelve months ago.

This year, I learned there's no replacement for the power of a hug and human connection.

I learned that laughter through tears is still my favorite emotion.

I learned—like many people—we can do great work from home.

I've seen friends who had to become schoolteachers for their kids. Teachers who had to keep students engaged and organized.

I learned that compassion has to start with yourself first, and only then can you have it for someone else.

I've learned that any change has to start from the inside. I finally get it when I hear Gandhi's words, 'Be the change you wish to see in the world.'

I learned that even in a year that was as difficult and challenging as this one, we still can find gratitude for the little things: coffee, text messages, friendship, and yoga pants. But only a year like this can make us drop to our knees in praise of toilet paper, sanitizer, masks, and curbside delivery.

Honestly… who knew in January we'd be grateful for a roll of Charmin? Not me.

And here we are, at the end of this historic point in time. It will surely go down in the record books for horrific statistics of illness and loss, but I'm going to try and keep my heart moving towards 2021, figuring out what this year meant to me. Everyone will carry with them a different memory and meaning, and that's okay. We are all different, and brave, and dealing with life the best we can.

I had to learn that too.

My wish for you to find peace, comfort, and joy in your daily life. Saving it for tomorrow is so 2020. Let's learn to live with it today… right here, right now.

Until next time, read something fabulous.

I LEARNED THAT COMPASSION HAS TO START WITH *yourself* FIRST, AND ONLY THEN CAN YOU HAVE IT FOR SOMEONE ELSE.

LIFE IS SHORT

This has been one of those weeks.

We lost a good friend, and nothing seems to make sense.

A wife. A mother. A sister. A daughter. A cousin. A friend. And yet, this barely scratches the surface of who she was.

She was so much to so many, and the fact that she went to bed one night and didn't wake up the next day is the hardest part to handle. I can't even imagine what her family is going through, and my heart goes out to each of them.

It's times like this that I really begin to look at my own life and re-evaluate choices that I make every day. I don't think there is anyone that heard about her and didn't question their own existence. When a death happens suddenly to someone so young, it's the ultimate wake-up call. It's the moment you realize you're either living the life of your dreams... or you're not.

Death has that sneaky way of giving everyone perspective and an immediate appreciation for life. You can use it to your advantage or simply let it slip by you and continue on with the life you're living.

It's totally up to you, and no one is judging.

It reminds me of the quote by Albert Einstein: "There are only two ways to live your life. One is as though nothing is a miracle. The other is as though everything is a miracle." We really do have the choice of how we view our own lives, and speaking from experience, my view could use a little work.

If you find yourself reading this, take stock of your life. Are you loved? Do you have family and friends who support you? Do you have reasons to wake up in the morning... even one? We—and by we, I mean me—take life so seriously and forget to look around at the abundance of love in our lives. I'm so guilty of living my life, stressed out by work or obligations, that I forget to see what is really around me. I think the only way to honor her, or any death, is to start seeing what is truly important at the end of the day.

Family. Friends. Love.

It's the hardest lesson to learn, but nothing else really matters, does it?

I think it's a lesson worth learning, and this is our wake-up call.

Take care, my friends. Life is short... Love hard. Be kind.

Family.

Friends.

Love.

IT'S THE HARDEST LESSON
TO LEARN, BUT NOTHING
ELSE REALLY MATTERS,
DOES IT?

DIG

This isn't what you think.

This is something better.

I know, I know… you came to this looking for answers, but the answers aren't always so clear and immediately at your disposal. There will be times when they are, and for that, you're welcome. More often than not, you will have to dig for the answers you are seeking. When I was a coach, I would often yell, "Dig, dig, dig," to the skaters, trying to get them to push themselves harder.

Dig.

That is what I have to tell myself too, but sadly not often enough. Lately, I have become complacent. Finding it easier to flip on Netflix than open the laptop. Zoning out is my newest winter pastime, but today I consider myself a student of finding out what I want. It's not sitting well with me to retreat, and I want to settle in with the feelings that have otherwise made me hide. Allowing all the angsty emotions to surface is a lesson in finding something better. It's no secret that my mind has a way of finding the darker side of any situation—often creating way more drama than is actually there.

I always thought it was just my writer's mind going to work.

But now I think it's a defect that needs to be addressed. Maybe "defect" is too strong of a word, but over the last few months, I've come to see the effects of my constant negative thoughts, and it isn't pretty.

In short, I needed to dig my way out of this hole.

The characters I created with the Frankfort series found a way to overcome the issues and circumstances I put them in, to rise above and create a new way of life for themselves. It wasn't easy for any of them—couldn't be if I wanted it to be authentic—but now I know what it truly takes to make changes. It's not something you can figure out in a weekend or a weekly planning session with yourself.

It's daily.

No, it's more than that.

Sometimes it's minute by minute, and eventually on the hour.

What I'm getting at is this requires a constant awareness you will have to maintain, if you truly want something to change. You also have to have a crystal-clear vision of what you do want. Health, wealth, or a better job? Do you want to write a book or start a blog? To be in a loving relationship? Everyone wants something, but not everyone allows themselves to dream.

I've given you that permission.

Take it and run. See what it is that you really want. It is time to finally let go of all the things that are holding you back. Let go of the past and all the negativity attached to it.

It's time to fall in love again. With your choices. With who you are. Yes, even with the baggage. Begin to look at your faults not as faults, but rather as the opposite of what you truly want in your life. As Jerry boldly said to George, "If every instinct you have is wrong, then the opposite would have to be right."

Take a moment today and think about something that's been bothering you. Now, flip it upside down and imagine exactly how you would like to see it instead. What steps can you take today? Tomorrow? It isn't about immediate resolution—just something to feel better about it now. It's about taking action and digging in, one scoop at a time.

Oddly enough, this is exactly how I process writing a book.

Start with a problem. (beginning)

What is the opposite or resolution? (ending)

How do I get from beginning to the end? (middle)

Simplistic for sure, and obviously, that pesky middle part is quite time-consuming. However, in keeping it simple like this, I know that plotting it out won't take me forever. Every author has their way of creating a story, and I have learned that this works for me. *Write Your Novel from the Middle* by James Scott Bell is an excellent resource for plotting this way, if you want more information.

Okay! So we're solving our own problems and applying it to plotting a book. Win-win! I told you writing would help you figure out how to live in this world. See what I did there?

IT'S TIME TO
FALL IN LOVE AGAIN.
WITH YOUR CHOICES.
WITH WHO YOU ARE.

Yes, even with the baggage.

WHY

"Faith is taking the first step even when you don't see the whole staircase."

— Martin Luther King Jr.

Since I published my first book, here is a list of questions I get almost on a daily basis:

How did you get into writing?

Where do you find the time?

Where do your ideas come from?

On and on... so many questions. And while I don't claim to have all the answers, I do have some ideas I'd like to share with you if writing might be your thing. I want this to be a place where everyone is welcome, and you walk away feeling inspired to try something new.

No one starts out writing their perfect novel on day one. It's writing exercises, blogging, and reading until your eyes are blurry. Some of you already have that going for you. The best thing you can do for your writing is read as much as possible. Not just your favorite genre, but anything that interests you.

A N Y T H I N G.

The only rule I have for your adventure is this: Be true to yourself.

Your writing doesn't have to be for anyone, or you might want it to be for everyone. The only person you have to answer to is yourself. Figure out why you want to do this, and once that is done, go for it.

The WHY is going to be different for all of us, and it will most likely change over the years. I always knew I wanted to be a writer but never really knew why until I started blogging and found helping others feel better about themselves made me incredibly happy.

Even when I only had a couple readers.

That didn't matter to me, and honestly still doesn't. What matters most is the impact I have on people and if I'm improving the quality of their lives. If I'm bringing them some hope or joy in any way, then I'm happy.

That has never changed.

My other why—the one that has developed through publishing—is simply to challenge myself. I have always pushed myself to think outside the box (not easy for an introvert) and try to make any goal attainable. Writing a book to me was never a HUGE deal, because I approached it as *how can I do that*? Obviously, the short answer is "word by word," but even more than that, I broke down the process and started with a couple characters and a conflict.

I adored writing my first book so much, even knowing it would never see the light of day. Seeing all of it come together was better than anything I could've hoped for and made me even more excited about creating characters to love.

So, using some #MondayMotivation, I want to start posting for those of you interested in making writing a part of your life. No need to create any goals yet... just start thinking about it. Every post will leave you with some "homework" that will guide you along the way. More than anything, I hope every post will leave you with a feeling of inspiration to create something. Art is art, no matter what form it takes.

Homework: What is your why?

Make a list of books you love—your top 10 books of all time. What do they have in common? Same genre? Fast-

paced or slow and lyrical? No wrong answers here. Somewhere in your answers is your why. Journal or think about it.
Give some thought as to why you're drawn to the books you
love above all others. You don't have to share your list with
anyone—unless you want to! Again, this workshop is strictly
for YOU, and you make the rules.

_____

_____

_____

_____

_____

_____

_____

_____

_____

_____

_____

_____

_____

_____

_____

_____

_____

_____

THE ONLY RULE I HAVE FOR YOUR ADVENTURE IS THIS:

Be true to yourself.

NOW

Have you ever felt like the universe was trying to tell you something? A word or topic will pop up over and over again, until you finally say, "OKAY, I get it. Thanks for the reminder."

Since the beginning of January, this word has been hounding me:

Now.

Not before. Not later.

Now.

As in, stop thinking about what happened last week, last month, or last year.

As in, stop playing out the worst-case scenario in your head.

As in, how about you just sit in this moment, NOW, and try that on for size?

It's no secret I have the world's most distracted brain, and one of my goals this year is to learn to be more present. I have several meditation apps, and I know how much better I feel when I can clear out the clutter and just be.

Not as easy as it sounds.

As a writer, I trained myself on running away with a thought in my head and seeing how much drama I can instill into it. I blame years of watching *The Young and the Restless* for that fun fact.

The thing is, when I stop the crazy voice in my head who likes to point out all that's wrong (or could be) in my life, then I actually have a moment of peace. I suddenly have clarity about what writing project I'm working on. Even reading is more enjoyable, because my mind doesn't have to compete with the words on the page.

In other words, everything is better without the mental chatter.

The main reason I'm writing about this today is because any craft that you choose—whether it be writing, painting, or even yoga—all of them will benefit from having a clear mind. A mind that isn't hell-bent on seeing the worst all the time. A mind that notices how wonderful the cookies smell baking in the oven. A mind that notices the slant of the shadow from the sun shining through the window. A mind that's drawn into the most intriguing plot twist.

Again, this isn't easy. I highly recommend getting an app like Calm or Headspace—both are great and offer free trials. It won't happen overnight, but if you notice it a few times a day, then you're on your way to a better use of your mind. If you notice yourself getting worked up over a thought in your head, stop, and notice what is really going on around you. Instead, see if you can use your five senses to engage in the moment.

"Climb out of your mind and back into your body, even if it feels uncomfortable. Turn toward the feeling, not away from it. Treat yourself the way you would treat a small child who is lost—because that part of you is."
— Geneen Roth, *This Messy Magnificent Life: A Field Guide*

P.S. if you haven't read that book, do so. It's life-changing good.

I know this wasn't exactly a writing lesson, but rather a life-lesson. I love to offer both. And the fact that you are going to clear the clutter in your head, will only mean that you are going to be a better artist, not to mention human.

I will admit I had so much fun writing this post, mostly because I've managed to stay focused the entire time. When I write from this place of clarity, it's the most I can offer the world. And it feels pretty damn good.

IN OTHER
WORDS,
*EVERYTHING
IS BETTER*
WITHOUT THE
MENTAL
CHATTER.

10 FOR 40

I don't know anyone else like her.

Except maybe her mom.

So, for Jenny's ~~fortieth~~ twenty-ninth birthday, I am going to do one of my favorite writing prompts and present you with ten things I love about Jen.

1. She is one of the funniest people I know.

2. She does this eyebrow thing when she gives you a look... it is everything.

3. Her lawyer skills come in handy when I have legal issues in my books.

4. She isn't afraid to wear a pig suit to pick up her kids at school.

5. She can meme any picture in ten seconds or less. Usually less.

6. She let me watch her kids for three-plus years. (That's nine in triplet years if you're counting.)

7. Her ability to find the absolute perfect gift is, well... a gift.

8. When she reads one of my books, I get a Snapchat of most of the pages with the best comments. Nothing is more fun than reading my own book with her commentary.

9. She wore any skimpy skating costume we threw her way. #sorrynotsorry

10. Gifs are her love language.

Obviously, this is the tip of the iceberg, and you'll just never understand till you get to know her. My co-workers have learned that if I'm laughing in my office—alone—it's usually a text from Jen.

There is a phrase I've used sparingly over the years, and I only think it's fitting now.

1 universe,

9 planets,

204 countries,

809 islands,

7 seas,

and I had the privilege to meet you.

I think that sums it up perfectly.

HBD, Jen

1 UNIVERSE,
9 PLANETS,
204 COUNTRIES,
809 ISLANDS,
7 SEAS,

and I had the
privilege to meet you.

HOW IT'S GOING

Friday, December 31, 2021

I am going through the edits of this book—secretly horrified I've committed myself to this project—and feeling the worst kind of writer's regret. That moment I realized everyone is going to be reading these words in a few months is terrifying for me.

Honestly, it's shocking I've published anything at all with this fear lurking in the background.

But, I'll take a deep breath (some call it a long sigh) and move forward.

Go—to quote Natalie in a past book. That one-word sentence that still motivates me.

Go. Go. *Go*!

Like any great recipe, writing a book has to have certain essential ingredients:

One cup theme.

Two-parts great characters. The cringier, the better.

Two-thirds cup of conflict.

A pinch of hope.

A dash of courage.

Mix it all in with an abundance of commitment and determination.

It's a recipe I've tried to rework with almost every book, and I come back to the same fear every single time. The reasons why I write fly out the window, and the fear sinks its claws into me like a cat on a brand-new sofa.

In my heart, I know what the reality is: These words mean very little in the grand scheme of life. A book is just a book.

It's not who I am, and while it may give you a glimpse inside my brain, it will always be just a part of me at a given time.

We change.

We evolve.

What I wrote about ten, twenty years ago is far different from what I write about now. And this book is the closest thing to a memoir of my early motherhood years as anything I'll ever write.

The one thing that never changes is that feeling of inadequacy that I believe all mothers (women? writers?) feel. If the only thing you ever learn from me is the bone-deep understanding that you are not alone, then I have accomplished what I set out to do.

What you're going through is normal.

How you are feeling matters.

Your dreams are everything.

You really can conquer whatever you set your mind to do.

Just like Glinda the Good Witch said to Dorothy, "You always had the power, my dear, you just had to learn it for yourself."

We are all here to learn, grow, and love.

Feel the fear, and do it anyway.

And when in doubt, read something fabulous.

xo, *mj*

IF THE ONLY
THING YOU EVER
LEARN FROM ME
IS THE BONE-DEEP
UNDERSTANDING
THAT <u>YOU ARE
NOT ALONE</u>,
THEN I HAVE
ACCOMPLISHED
WHAT I SET OUT
TO DO.

ACKNOWLEDGEMENTS

The true test of a good working relationship is being able to email your editor with this crazy idea that came to you on a car ride, and she responds ALL CAPS IN. Then, she sends you the *exact* cover you wanted the next day. You guys, she is my biggest cheerleader and fan, and I am so grateful to have her in the car with me as I drive down this crazy path. Susie, I've said it before, but thank you just never seems big enough. I adore working with you.

The challenge of finding inspiration is you need to know where to look. For some it's music, while others find it in nature.

Okay, *most* people can find inspiration in nature.

The trick is figuring out what does work for you, and then consciously building that into your world. I'm lucky, and have always found real life to be inspiring. Our brilliance isn't in how perfect we can make our lives... It's how we can appreciate the imperfections in our lives.

As you can see from the previous pages, I have made it a mission to find a bright side in any situation, but if it wasn't for my family and friends, readers and co-workers, none of it would've been possible.

I created Dream Life Publications, not because I want you all to have perfect lives. Just the opposite. I want you to love the life you have, and to stop comparing your insides to someone else's outside. My mission is to bring you some joy and laughter into your perfectly imperfect world, and the only way that happens is by creating more books for you to love.

You, my dear readers, are my inspiration.

You always have been.

So, thank you for continuing to allow me into your hearts.

We're just getting started.

UNTIL NEXT TIME, READ SOMETHING FABULOUS...

Bird by Bird by Anne Lamott

This Messy Magnificent Life by Geneen Roth

You are a Badass by Jen Sincero

Write Your Novel from the Middle by James Scott Bell

Pen on Fire by Barbara Demarco-Barrett

The High 5 Habit by Mel Robbins

Year of Yes by Shonda Rhimes

The Life List by Lori Nelson Spielman

Atomic Habits by James Clear

The War of Art by Steven Pressfield

The Gifts of Imperfection by Brené Brown

Made in the USA
Monee, IL
23 July 2022

10192954R00095